Bible Promises
to Treasure
for Men

Inspiring

words

for every

occasion

BROADMAN
&HOLMAN
PUBLISHERS

Nashville, Tennessee

Bible Promises

to Treasure

for Men

Bible Promises to Treasure for Men
©1998 Broadman & Holman Publishers,
Nashville, Tennessee
All rights reserved
Printed in Belgium

ISBN 0-8054-9328-X

Dewey Decimal Classification: 248.8
Subject Heading: CHRISTIAN MEN

******

A note on the sources of quotations. When possible I have supplied at least the book name from which contemporary quotes have come. Yet even this is often impossible, since many came from my "journal of jottings" over many years. Also, if a quote is from a person who lived longer than fifty or so years ago, I've made no attempt to cite the source. Such quotations are usually available in any standard book of quotes.

******

Library of Congress Cataloging-in-Publication Data
Bible promises to treasure for men : inspiring words for every
  occasion / compiled by Gary Wilde.
      p. cm.
    Includes bibliographical references.
    ISBN 0-8054-9328-X
    1. Christian men—Religious life—Quotations. 2. Christian
  life—Quotations maxims, etc. I. Wilde, Gary
  BV4528.2B53   1999
  248.8'42—dc21   98-36038
                                                         CIP

1 2 3 4 5 6 02 01 00 99 98

Contents

Introduction

I remember as a child singing often at church: "Standing on the Promises of God." Or maybe it was mostly the adults who were singing; but I was standing next to them—my parents and all the others. I recall those faithful people joyfully reciting words they must surely have known by heart . . .

**When the howling storms
of doubt and fear assail,
By the living Word of God I shall prevail,
Standing on the promises of God.**

For years Downey Church, in sunny central Florida, had preached and taught the promises of God and believed in His goodness. From the beginning—when the church building was a small tin-roofed, A-frame at the east end of a dirt road on the outskirts of Orlando—people

1

would gather to stand on the immutable promises. Under the shiny tin roof, standing on the sandy-wooden floorboards, they melded their voices to the tunes of the upright piano and recalled God's goodness. Today, as the church there grows and thrives—now there is also a school and gymnasium—I can only attribute its vibrant life to a love of God's promises and the recognition that without the pledges that flow from the mouth of God, there is no church, no music, and no reason for either.

The promises of God have always been the bedrock of Christian faith; for without God's sacred covenants with us, we cannot survive. In times of joy or heartache, in all our ups and downs, we keep coming back to that source of our life: the motivation for all our doing and the reason for our existence. It is the message of God's mighty assurances: this life is not all there is, He will always be with us while we are here, and He will take us to be with Him someday. Yes, we do have priceless promises to keep close to our hearts!

My hope for you as you delve into this scriptural treasure chest is that you will grow deeper in love with the One who has spoken as no other ever could. With so many influences bombarding our minds each moment of the day, what could be better than to set aside a few moments of quiet to hear the still, small voice that constantly invites us into warm fellowship? We'll be richly rewarded if we truly listen to what that voice is saying. His words convey blessing and guidance, wisdom and warning, life for now and life everlasting. What incomparable grace!

Gary Wilde
Oviedo, Florida, 1998

One

Where Do I Find Some Good Role Models?

We all need people to look up to, no matter how old we are. Men, especially, look for mentors who can show them how to live and work and grow in the spiritual life. Why not look to the Bible first?

Here Are Your Biblical Mentors . . .

Other men are lenses through which we read our own minds.

—*Ralph Waldo Emerson*

He that walketh with wise men shall be wise: but a companion of fools shall be destroyed.

—*Proverbs 13:20*

Abraham: Stepping Out in Faith

Now the LORD had said unto Abram, Get thee out of thy country, and from thy kindred, and from thy father's house, unto a land that I will shew thee:

And I will make of thee a great nation, and I will bless thee, and make thy name great; and thou shalt be a blessing:

And I will bless them that bless thee, and curse him that curseth thee: and in thee shall all families of the earth be blessed.

So Abram departed, as the LORD had spoken unto him; and Lot went with him: and Abram was seventy and five years old when he departed out of Haran.

And Abram took Sarai his wife, and Lot his brother's son, and all their substance that they had gathered, and the souls that they had gotten in Haran; and they went forth to go into the land of Canaan; and into the land of Canaan they came.

And Abram passed through the land unto the place of Sichem, unto the plain of Moreh. And the Canaanite was then in the land.

And the LORD appeared unto Abram, and said, Unto thy seed will I give this land: and there builded he an altar unto the LORD, who appeared unto him.

And he removed from thence unto a mountain on the east of Beth–el, and pitched his tent, having Beth–el on the west, and Hai on the east: and there he builded an altar unto the LORD, and called upon the name of the LORD.

And Abram journeyed, going on still toward the south.

—Genesis 12:1–9

Asa: Doing the Right Thing

And in the twentieth year of Jeroboam king of Israel reigned Asa over Judah.

And forty and one years reigned he in Jerusalem. And his mother's name was Maachah, the daughter of Abishalom.

And Asa did that which was right in the eyes of the LORD, as did David his father.

And he took away the sodomites out of the land, and removed all the idols that his fathers had made.

And also Maachah his mother, even her he removed from being queen, because she had made an idol in a grove; and Asa destroyed her idol, and burnt it by the brook Kidron.

But the high places were not removed: nevertheless Asa's heart was perfect with the LORD all his days.

And he brought in the things which his father had dedicated, and the things which himself had dedicated, into the house of the LORD, silver, and gold, and vessels.

—*1 Kings 15:9–15*

Gideon: Doing What God Commanded

And it came to pass the same night, that the LORD said unto him, Take thy father's young bullock, even the second bullock of seven years old, and throw down the altar of Baal that thy father hath, and cut down the grove that is by it:

And build an altar unto the LORD thy God upon the top of this rock, in the ordered place, and take the second bullock, and offer a burnt sacrifice with the wood of the grove which thou shalt cut down.

Then Gideon took ten men of his servants, and did as the LORD had said unto him: and so it was, because he feared his father's household, and the men of the city, that he could not do it by day, that he did it by night.

And when the men of the city arose early in the morning, behold, the altar of Baal was cast down, and the grove was cut down that was by it, and the second bullock was offered upon the altar that was built.

And they said one to another, Who hath done this thing? And when they inquired and asked, they said, Gideon the son of Joash hath done this thing.

Then the men of the city said unto Joash, Bring out thy son, that he may die: because he hath cast down the altar of Baal, and because he hath cut down the grove that was by it.

And Joash said unto all that stood against him, Will ye plead for Baal? will ye save him? he that will plead for him, let him be put to death whilst it is yet morning: if he be a god, let him plead for himself, because one hath cast down his altar.

—Judges 6:25–31

Joshua and Caleb: Withstanding Popular Opinion

And Joshua the son of Nun, and Caleb the son of Jephunneh, which were of them that searched the land, rent their clothes:

And they spake unto all the company of the children of Israel, saying, The land, which we passed through to search it, is an exceeding good land.

If the LORD delight in us, then he will bring us into this land, and give it us; a land which floweth with milk and honey.

Only rebel not ye against the LORD, neither fear ye the people of the land; for they are bread for us: their defence is departed from them, and the LORD is with us: fear them not.

But all the congregation bade stone them with stones. And the glory of the LORD appeared in the tabernacle of the congregation before all the children of Israel.

And the LORD said unto Moses, How long will this people provoke me? and how long will it be ere they believe me, for all the signs which I have shewed among them?

I will smite them with the pestilence, and disinherit them, and will make of thee a greater nation and mightier than they.

—*Numbers 14:6–12*

Joshua: Willing to Trust God

Now after the death of Moses the servant of the LORD it came to pass, that the LORD spake unto Joshua the son of Nun, Moses' minister, saying,

Moses my servant is dead; now therefore arise, go over this Jordan, thou, and all this people, unto the land which I do give to them, even to the children of Israel.

Every place that the sole of your foot shall tread upon, that have I given unto you, as I said unto Moses.

From the wilderness and this Lebanon even unto the great river, the river Euphrates, all the land of the Hittites, and unto the great sea toward the going down of the sun, shall be your coast.

There shall not any man be able to stand before thee all the days of thy life: as I was with Moses, so I will be with thee: I will not fail thee, nor forsake thee.

Be strong and of a good courage: for unto this people shalt thou divide for an inheritance the land, which I sware unto their fathers to give them.

Only be thou strong and very courageous, that thou mayest observe to do according to all the law, which Moses my servant commanded thee: turn not from it to the right hand or to the left, that thou mayest prosper whithersoever thou goest.

This book of the law shall not depart out of thy mouth; but thou shalt meditate therein day and night, that thou mayest observe to do according to all that is written therein: for then thou shalt make thy way prosperous, and then thou shalt have good success.

Have not I commanded thee? Be strong and of a good courage; be not afraid, neither be thou dismayed: for the LORD thy God is with thee whithersoever thou goest.

Then Joshua commanded the officers of the people, saying,

Pass through the host, and command the people, saying, Prepare you victuals; for within three days ye shall pass over this Jordan, to go in to possess the land, which the LORD your God giveth you to possess it.

—*Joshua 1:1–11*

And Joshua gathered all the tribes of Israel to Shechem, and called for the elders of Israel, and for their heads, and for their judges, and for their officers; and they presented themselves before God.

And Joshua said unto all the people, Thus saith the LORD God of Israel, Your fathers dwelt on the other side of the flood in old time, even Terah, the father of Abraham, and the father of Nachor: and they served other gods. . . .

Now therefore fear the LORD, and serve him in sincerity and in truth: and put away the gods which your fathers served on the other side of the flood, and in Egypt; and serve ye the LORD.

And if it seem evil unto you to serve the LORD, choose you this day whom ye will serve; whether the gods which your fathers served that were on the other side of the flood, or the gods of the Amorites, in whose land ye dwell: but as for me and my house, we will serve the LORD.

—*Joshua 24:1–2, 14–15*

✒ *Joseph: Able to Forgive*

Then Joseph could not refrain himself before all them that stood by him; and he cried, Cause every man to go out from me. And there stood no man with him, while Joseph made himself known unto his brethren.

And he wept aloud: and the Egyptians and the house of Pharaoh heard.

And Joseph said unto his brethren, I am Joseph; doth my father yet live? And his brethren could not answer him; for they were troubled at his presence.

And Joseph said unto his brethren, Come near to me, I pray you. And they came near. And he said I am Joseph your brother, whom ye sold into Egypt.

Now therefore be not grieved, nor angry with yourselves, that ye sold me hither: for God did send me before you to preserve life.

—*Genesis 45:1–5*

David: Ready to Repent

And the LORD sent Nathan unto David. And he came unto him, and said unto him, There were two men in one city; the one rich, and the other poor.

The rich man had exceeding many flocks and herds:

But the poor man had nothing, save one little ewe lamb, which he had bought and nourished up: and it grew up together with him, and with his children; it did eat of his own meat, and drank of his own cup, and lay in his bosom, and was unto him as a daughter.

And there came a traveller unto the rich man, and he spared to take of his own flock and of his own herd, to dress for the wayfaring man that was come unto him; but took the poor man's lamb, and dressed it for the man that was come to him.

And David's anger was greatly kindled against the man; and he said to Nathan, As the LORD liveth, the man that hath done this thing shall surely die:

And he shall restore the lamb fourfold, because he did this thing, and because he had no pity.

And Nathan said to David, Thou art the man. Thus saith the LORD God of Israel, I anointed thee king over Israel, and I delivered thee out of the hand of Saul;

And I gave thee thy master's house, and thy master's wives into thy bosom, and gave thee the house of Israel and of Judah; and if that had been too little, I would moreover have given unto thee such and such things.

Wherefore hast thou despised the commandment of the LORD, to do evil in his sight? thou hast killed Uriah the Hittite with the sword, and hast taken his wife to be thy wife, and hast slain him with the sword of the children of Ammon.

Now therefore the sword shall never depart from thine house; because thou hast despised me, and hast taken the wife of Uriah the Hittite to be thy wife.

Thus saith the LORD, Behold, I will raise up evil against thee out of thine own house, and I will take thy wives before thine eyes, and give them unto thy neighbour, and he shall lie with thy wives in the sight of this sun.

For thou didst it secretly: but I will do this thing before all Israel, and before the sun.

And David said unto Nathan, I have sinned against the LORD.

—*2 Samuel 12:1–13*

℘Daniel: Standing Up to Persecution

Now when Daniel knew that the writing was signed, he went into his house; and his windows being open in his chamber toward Jerusalem, he kneeled upon his knees three times a day, and prayed, and gave thanks before his God, as he did aforetime.

Then these men assembled, and found Daniel praying and making supplication before his God.

Then they came near, and spake before the king concerning the king's decree; Hast thou not signed a decree, that every man that shall ask a petition of any God or man within thirty days, save of thee, O king, shall

be cast into the den of lions? The king
answered and said, The thing is true,
according to the law of the Medes and
Persians, which altereth not.

Then answered they and said before the
king, That Daniel, which is of the children
of the captivity of Judah, regardeth not thee,
O king, nor the decree that thou hast
signed, but maketh his petition three times
a day.

Then the king, when he heard these
words, was sore displeased with himself, and
set his heart on Daniel to deliver him: and
he laboured till the going down of the sun
to deliver him.

Then these men assembled unto the king,
and said unto the king, Know, O king, that
the law of the Medes and Persians is, That
no decree nor statute which the king
establisheth may be changed.

Then the king commanded, and they
brought Daniel, and cast him into the den
of lions. Now the king spake and said unto
Daniel, Thy God whom thou servest
continually, he will deliver thee.

And a stone was brought and laid upon the mouth of the den; and the king sealed it with his own signet, and with the signet of his lords; that the purpose might not be changed concerning Daniel.

Then the king went to his palace, and passed the night fasting: neither were instruments of musick brought before him: and his sleep went from him.

Then the king arose very early in the morning, and went in haste unto the den of lions.

And when he came to the den, he cried with a lamentable voice unto Daniel: and the king spake and said to Daniel, O Daniel, servant of the living God, is thy God, whom thou servest continually, able to deliver thee from the lions?

Then said Daniel unto the king, O king, live for ever.

My God hath sent his angel, and hath shut the lions' mouths, that they have not hurt me: forasmuch as before him innocency was found in me; and also before thee, O king, have I done no hurt.

Then was the king exceeding glad for him, and commanded that they should take Daniel up out of the den. So Daniel was taken up out of the den, and no manner of hurt was found upon him, because he believed in his God.

—Daniel 6:10–23

Three Hebrews: Showing Incredible Courage

Shadrach, Meshach, and Abed–nego, answered and said to the king, O Nebuchadnezzar, we are not careful to answer thee in this matter.

If it be so, our God whom we serve is able to deliver us from the burning fiery furnace, and he will deliver us out of thine hand, O king.

But if not, be it known unto thee, O king, that we will not serve thy gods, nor worship the golden image which thou hast set up.

—Daniel 3:16–18

❧Nehemiah: Overcoming Discouragement

Afterward I came unto the house of Shemaiah the son of Delaiah the son of Mehetabeel, who was shut up; and he said, Let us meet together in the house of God, within the temple, and let us shut the doors of the temple: for they will come to slay thee; yea, in the night will they come to slay thee.

And I said, Should such a man as I flee? and who is there, that, being as I am, would go into the temple to save his life? I will not go in.

And, lo, I perceived that God had not sent him; but that he pronounced this prophecy against me: for Tobiah and Sanballat had hired him.

Therefore was he hired, that I should be afraid, and do so, and sin, and that they might have matter for an evil report, that they might reproach me.

—*Nehemiah 6:10–13*

Paul and the Disciples: Testifying with Courage

Now when Paul and his company loosed from Paphos, they came to Perga in Pamphylia: and John departing from them returned to Jerusalem.

But when they departed from Perga, they came to Antioch in Pisidia, and went into the synagogue on the sabbath day, and sat down.

And after the reading of the law and the prophets the rulers of the synagogue sent unto them, saying, Ye men and brethren, if ye have any word of exhortation for the people, say on.

Then Paul stood up, and beckoning with his hand said, Men of Israel, and ye that fear God, give audience.

—Acts 13:13–16

And how I kept back nothing that was profitable unto you, but have shewed you, and have taught you publickly, and from house to house,

Testifying both to the Jews, and also to the Greeks, repentance toward God, and faith toward our Lord Jesus Christ.

And now, behold, I go bound in the spirit unto Jerusalem, not knowing the things that shall befall me there:

Save that the Holy Ghost witnesseth in every city, saying that bonds and afflictions abide me.

But none of these things move me, neither count I my life dear unto myself, so that I might finish my course with joy, and the ministry, which I have received of the Lord Jesus, to testify the gospel of the grace of God.

—Acts 20:20–24

✐ Philip: Witnessing for Christ

The day following Jesus would go forth into Galilee, and findeth Philip, and saith unto him, Follow me.

Now Philip was of Bethsaida, the city of Andrew and Peter.

Philip findeth Nathanael, and saith unto him, We have found him, of whom Moses in the law, and the prophets, did write, Jesus of Nazareth, the son of Joseph.

And Nathanael said unto him, Can there any good thing come out of Nazareth? Philip saith unto him, Come and see.

Jesus saw Nathanael coming to him, and saith of him, Behold an Israelite indeed, in whom is no guile!

Nathanael saith unto him, Whence knowest thou me? Jesus answered and said unto him, Before that Philip called thee, when thou wast under the fig tree, I saw thee.

Nathanael answered and saith unto him, Rabbi, thou art the Son of God; thou art the King of Israel.

Jesus answered and said unto him, Because I said unto thee, I saw thee under the fig tree, believest thou? thou shalt see greater things than these.

And he saith unto him, Verily, verily, I say unto you, Hereafter ye shall see heaven open, and the angels of God ascending and descending upon the Son of man.

—*John 1:43–51*

And the angel of the Lord spake unto Philip, saying, Arise, and go toward the south unto the way that goeth down from Jerusalem unto Gaza, which is desert.

And he arose and went: and, behold, a man of Ethiopia, an eunuch of great authority under Candace queen of the Ethiopians, who had the charge of all her treasure, and had come to Jerusalem for to worship,

Was returning, and sitting in his chariot read Esaias the prophet.

Then the Spirit said unto Philip, Go near, and join thyself to this chariot.

And Philip ran thither to him, and heard him read the prophet Esaias, and said, Understandest thou what thou readest?

And he said, How can I, except some man should guide me? And he desired Philip that he would come up and sit with him.

The place of the scripture which he read was this, He was led as a sheep to the slaughter; and like a lamb dumb before his shearer, so opened he not his mouth:

In his humiliation his judgment was taken away: and who shall declare his generation? for his life is taken from the earth.

And the eunuch answered Philip, and said, I pray thee, of whom speaketh the prophet this? of himself, or of some other man?

Then Philip opened his mouth, and began at the same scripture, and preached unto him Jesus.

And as they went on their way, they came unto a certain water: and the eunuch said, See, here is water; what doth hinder me to be baptized?

And Philip said, If thou believest with all thine heart, thou mayest. And he answered and said, I believe that Jesus Christ is the Son of God.

And he commanded the chariot to stand still: and they went down both into the water, both Philip and the eunuch; and he baptized him.

And when they were come up out of the water, the Spirit of the Lord caught away Philip, that the eunuch saw him no more: and he went on his way rejoicing.

—Acts 8:26–39

Timothy: Being a Teachable Man

Let no man despise thy youth; but be thou an example of the believers, in word, in conversation, in charity, in spirit, in faith, in purity.

—*1 Timothy 4:12*

Paul, an apostle of Jesus Christ by the will of God, according to the promise of life which is in Christ Jesus,

To Timothy, my dearly beloved son: Grace, mercy, and peace, from God the Father and Christ Jesus our Lord.

I thank God, whom I serve from my forefathers with pure conscience, that without ceasing I have remembrance of thee in my prayers night and day;

Greatly desiring to see thee, being mindful of thy tears, that I may be filled with joy;

When I call to remembrance the unfeigned faith that is in thee, which dwelt first in thy grandmother Lois, and thy mother Eunice; and I am persuaded that in thee also.

Wherefore I put thee in remembrance that thou stir up the gift of God, which is in thee by the putting on of my hands.

For God hath not given us the spirit of fear; but of power, and of love, and of a sound mind.

—*2 Timothy 1:1–7*

Thou therefore, my son, be strong in the grace that is in Christ Jesus.

And the things that thou hast heard of me among many witnesses, the same commit thou to faithful men, who shall be able to teach others also.

Thou therefore endure hardness, as a good soldier of Jesus Christ.

No man that warreth entangleth himself with the affairs of this life; that he may please him who hath chosen him to be a soldier.

And if a man also strive for masteries, yet is he not crowned, except he strive lawfully.

The husbandman that laboureth must be first partaker of the fruits.

Consider what I say; and the Lord give thee understanding in all things.

Remember that Jesus Christ of the seed of David was raised from the dead according to my gospel:

Wherein I suffer trouble, as an evil doer, even unto bonds; but the word of God is not bound.

Therefore I endure all things for the elect's sakes, that they may also obtain the salvation which is in Christ Jesus with eternal glory.

It is a faithful saying: For if we be dead with him, we shall also live with him:

If we suffer, we shall also reign with him: if we deny him, he also will deny us:

If we believe not, yet he abideth faithful: he cannot deny himself.

—*2 Timothy 2:1–13*

But thou hast fully known my doctrine, manner of life, purpose, faith, longsuffering, charity, patience,

Persecutions, afflictions, which came unto me at Antioch, at Iconium, at Lystra;

what persecutions I endured: but out of
them all the Lord delivered me.

—2 Timothy 3:10–11

Watch Out Whom You Follow!

*Virtuous men do good by setting themselves
up as models before the public. But I do good
by setting myself up as a warning.*

—Michel de Montaigne

Verily, verily, I say unto you, He that
entereth not by the door into the sheepfold,
but climbeth up some other way, the same
is a thief and a robber.

But he that entereth in by the door is the
shepherd of the sheep.

To him the porter openeth; and the sheep
hear his voice: and he calleth his own sheep
by name, and leadeth them out.

And when he putteth forth his own
sheep, he goeth before them, and the sheep
follow him: for they know his voice.

And a stranger will they not follow, but will flee from him: for they know not the voice of strangers.

This parable spake Jesus unto them: but they understood not what things they were which he spake unto them.

Then said Jesus unto them again, Verily, verily, I say unto you, I am the door of the sheep.

All that ever came before me are thieves and robbers: but the sheep did not hear them.

I am the door: by me if any man enter in, he shall be saved, and shall go in and out, and find pasture.

The thief cometh not, but for to steal, and to kill, and to destroy: I am come that they might have life, and that they might have it more abundantly.

I am the good shepherd: the good shepherd giveth his life for the sheep.

But he that is an hireling, and not the shepherd, whose own the sheep are not, seeth the wolf coming, and leaveth the sheep, and fleeth: and the wolf catcheth them, and scattereth the sheep.

The hireling fleeth, because he is an hireling, and careth not for the sheep.

—*John 10:1–13*

And art confident that thou thyself art a guide of the blind, a light of them which are in darkness,

An instructor of the foolish, a teacher of babes, which hast the form of knowledge and of the truth in the law.

Thou therefore which teachest another, teachest thou not thyself? thou that preachest a man should not steal, dost thou steal?

Thou that sayest a man should not commit adultery, dost thou commit adultery? thou that abhorrest idols, dost thou commit sacrilege?

Thou that makest thy boast of the law, through breaking the law dishonourest thou God?

For the name of God is blasphemed among the Gentiles through you, as it is written.

For circumcision verily profiteth, if thou keep the law: but if thou be a breaker of the

law, thy circumcision is made
uncircumcision.

—Romans 2:19–25

I marvel that ye are so soon removed
from him that called you into the grace of
Christ unto another gospel:

Which is not another; but there be some
that trouble you, and would pervert the
gospel of Christ.

But though we, or an angel from heaven,
preach any other gospel unto you than that
which we have preached unto you, let him
be accursed.

—Galatians 1:6–8

Beloved, believe not every spirit, but try
the spirits whether they are of God: because
many false prophets are gone out into the
world.

Hereby know ye the Spirit of God: Every
spirit that confesseth that Jesus Christ is
come in the flesh is of God:

And every spirit that confesseth not that
Jesus Christ is come in the flesh is not of
God: and this is that spirit of antichrist,

whereof ye have heard that it should come; and even now already is it in the world.

Ye are of God, little children, and have overcome them: because greater is he that is in you, than he that is in the world.

They are of the world: therefore speak they of the world, and the world heareth them.

—*1 John 4:1–5*

For many deceivers are entered into the world, who confess not that Jesus Christ is come in the flesh. This is a deceiver and an antichrist.

—*2 John 7*

Two

What Do I Do When the Going Gets Tough?

Where is the first place you turn when the hard times hit? To your spouse or parents? To a trusted friend or work colleague? Or do you simply gear up and turn inside—to your own "inner reserves" for strength to persevere? Any of these sources of support can help us. But God calls us to turn to Him first. He can work through all the circumstances and people in our lives; He's simply waiting to be invited.

Rely on God's Strength . . .

The longer I live, the more convincing proofs I see of this truth, that God governs in the affairs of man; and if a sparrow cannot fall to the ground without his notice, is it probable that an empire can rise without his aid?

—Benjamin Franklin

Such trust have we through Christ to God-ward:

Not that we are sufficient of ourselves to think any thing as of ourselves; but our sufficiency is of God.

—2 Corinthians 3:4–5

My help cometh from the LORD, which made heaven and earth.

He will not suffer thy foot to be moved: he that keepeth thee will not slumber.

—Psalm 121:2–3

Seeing then that we have a great high priest, that is passed into the heavens, Jesus the Son of God, let us hold fast our profession.

For we have not an high priest which cannot be touched with the feeling of our infirmities; but was in all points tempted like as we are, yet without sin.

Let us therefore come boldly unto the throne of grace, that we may obtain mercy, and find grace to help in time of need.

—Hebrews 4:14–16

I can do all things through Christ which strengtheneth me.

—Philippians 4:13

When You Struggle with Doubts

And he said, Come. And when Peter was come down out of the ship, he walked on the water, to go to Jesus.

But when he saw the wind boisterous, he was afraid; and beginning to sink, he cried, saying, Lord, save me.

And immediately Jesus stretched forth his hand, and caught him, and said unto him, O thou of little faith, wherefore didst thou doubt?

—Matthew 14:29–31

And the LORD looked upon him [Gideon], and said, Go in this thy might, and thou shalt save Israel from the hand of the Midianites: have not I sent thee?

And he said unto him, Oh my Lord, wherewith shall I save Israel? behold, my family is poor in Manasseh, and I am the least in my father's house.

And the LORD said unto him, Surely I will be with thee, and thou shalt smite the Midianites as one man.

—Judges 6:14–16

For I know that my redeemer liveth, and that he shall stand at the latter day upon the earth

And though after my skin worms destroy this body, yet in my flesh shall I see God:

Whom I shall see for myself, and mine eyes shall behold, and not another; though my reins be consumed within me.

—Job 19:25–27

Trust in the LORD with all thine heart; and lean not unto thine own understanding.

In all thy ways acknowledge him, and he shall direct thy paths.

—Proverbs 3:5–6

❧ *When You're Afraid*

Hearken unto me, ye that know righteousness, the people in whose heart is my law; fear ye not the reproach of men, neither be ye afraid of their revilings.

—Isaiah 51:7

The LORD is my light and my salvation; whom shall I fear? the LORD is the strength of my life; of whom shall I be afraid?

When the wicked, even mine enemies and my foes, came upon me to eat up my flesh, they stumbled and fell.

Though an host should encamp against me, my heart shall not fear: though war should rise against me, in this will I be confident.

—Psalm 27:1–3

Therefore will not we fear, though the earth be removed, and though the mountains be carried into the midst of the sea.

—Psalm 46:2

For God hath not given us the spirit of fear; but of power, and of love, and of a sound mind.

—2 Timothy 1:7

There is no fear in love; but perfect love casteth out fear: because fear hath torment. He that feareth is not made perfect in love.

—1 John 4:18

When You're Frustrated

My soul is weary of my life; I will leave my complaint upon myself; I will speak in the bitterness of my soul.

I will say unto God, Do not condemn me; shew me wherefore thou contendest with me.

Is it good unto thee that thou shouldest oppress, that thou shouldest despise the work of thine hands, and shine upon the counsel of the wicked?

Hast thou eyes of flesh? or seest thou as man seeth?

Are thy days as the days of man? are thy years as man's days,

That thou inquirest after mine iniquity, and searchest after my sin?

Thou knowest that I am not wicked; and there is none that can deliver out of thine hand.

Thine hands have made me and fashioned me together round about; yet thou dost destroy me.

Remember, I beseech thee, that thou hast made me as the clay; and wilt thou bring me into dust again?

—*Job 10:1–9*

I will lift up mine eyes unto the hills, from whence cometh my help.

My help cometh from the LORD, which made heaven and earth.

He will not suffer thy foot to be moved: he that keepeth thee will not slumber.

Behold, he that keepeth Israel shall neither slumber nor sleep.

The LORD is thy keeper: the LORD is thy shade upon thy right hand.

The sun shall not smite thee by day, nor the moon by night.

The LORD shall preserve thee from all evil: he shall preserve thy soul.

The LORD shall preserve thy going out and thy coming in from this time forth, and even for evermore.

—*Psalm 121*

When You're Feeling Exhausted

Have mercy upon me, O LORD; for I am weak: O LORD, heal me; for my bones are vexed.

My soul is also sore vexed: but thou, O LORD, how long?

—Psalm 6:2–3

So I returned, and considered all the oppressions that are done under the sun: and behold the tears of such as were oppressed, and they had no comforter; and on the side of their oppressors there was power; but they had no comforter.

Wherefore I praised the dead which are already dead more than the living which are yet alive.

—Ecclesiastes 4:1–2

He giveth power to the faint; and to them that have no might he increaseth strength.

Even the youths shall faint and be weary, and the young men shall utterly fall:

But they that wait upon the LORD shall renew their strength; they shall mount up with wings as eagles; they shall run, and not be weary; and they shall walk, and not faint.

—Isaiah 40:29–31

Come unto me, all ye that labour and are heavy laden, and I will give you rest.

Take my yoke upon you, and learn of me; for I am meek and lowly in heart: and ye shall find rest unto your souls.

For my yoke is easy, and my burden is light.

—Matthew 11:28–30

When You're Overwhelmed with Worry

I say unto you, Take no thought for your life, what ye shall eat, or what ye shall drink; nor yet for your body, what ye shall put on. Is not the life more than meat, and the body than raiment?

Behold the fowls of the air: for they sow not, neither do they reap, nor gather into barns; yet your heavenly Father feedeth them. Are ye not much better than they?

Which of you by taking thought can add one cubit unto his stature?

And why take ye thought for raiment? Consider the lilies of the field, how they grow; they toil not, neither do they spin:

And yet I say unto you, That even Solomon in all his glory was not arrayed like one of these.

Wherefore, if God so clothe the grass of the field, which to day is, and to morrow is cast into the oven, shall he not much more clothe you, O ye of little faith?

Therefore take no thought, saying, What shall we eat? or, What shall we drink? or, Wherewithal shall we be clothed?

(For after all these things do the Gentiles seek:) for your heavenly Father knoweth that ye have need of all these things.

But seek ye first the kingdom of God, and his righteousness; and all these things shall be added unto you.

Take therefore no thought for the morrow: for the morrow shall take thought for the things of itself. Sufficient unto the day is the evil thereof.

—Matthew 6:25–34

Thou wilt keep him in perfect peace, whose mind is stayed on thee: because he trusteth in thee.

—*Isaiah 26:3*

For he shall be as a tree planted by the waters, and that spreadeth out her roots by the river, and shall not see when heat cometh, but her leaf shall be green; and shall not be careful in the year of drought, neither shall cease from yielding fruit.

—*Jeremiah 17:8*

Now the Lord of peace himself give you peace always by all means. The Lord be with you all.

—*2 Thessalonians 3:16*

When You're Dealing with Failure

The LORD is nigh unto them that are of a broken heart; and saveth such as be of a contrite spirit.

—*Psalm 34:18*

Commit thy works unto the LORD, and
thy thoughts shall be established.

—Proverbs 16:3

But none of these things move me,
neither count I my life dear unto myself, so
that I might finish my course with joy, and
the ministry, which I have received of the
Lord Jesus, to testify the gospel of the grace
of God.

—Acts 20:24

But we have this treasure in earthen
vessels, that the excellency of the power may
be of God, and not of us.

We are troubled on every side, yet not
distressed; we are perplexed, but not in
despair;

Persecuted, but not forsaken; cast down,
but not destroyed;

Always bearing about in the body the
dying of the Lord Jesus, that the life also of
Jesus might be made manifest in our body.

For we which live are alway delivered
unto death for Jesus' sake, that the life also

of Jesus might be made manifest in our mortal flesh.

—*2 Corinthians 4:7–11*

When You're Tense and Stressed-Out

In the day of my trouble I sought the Lord: my sore ran in the night, and ceased not: my soul refused to be comforted.

I remembered God, and was troubled: I complained, and my spirit was overwhelmed.

Thou holdest mine eyes waking: I am so troubled that I cannot speak.

I have considered the days of old, the years of ancient times.

I call to remembrance my song in the night: I commune with mine own heart: and my spirit made diligent search.

—*Psalm 77:2–6*

All things are for your sakes, that the abundant grace might through the thanksgiving of many redound to the glory of God.

For which cause we faint not; but though our outward man perish, yet the inward man is renewed day by day.

For our light affliction, which is but for a moment, worketh for us a far more exceeding and eternal weight of glory;

While we look not at the things which are seen, but at the things which are not seen: for the things which are seen are temporal; but the things which are not seen are eternal.

—2 Corinthians 4:15–18

Rejoice evermore.

Pray without ceasing.

In every thing give thanks: for this is the will of God in Christ Jesus concerning you.

—1 Thessalonians 5:16–18

Who shall also confirm you unto the end, that ye may be blameless in the day of our Lord Jesus Christ.

God is faithful, by whom ye were called unto the fellowship of his Son Jesus Christ our Lord.

—1 Corinthians 1:8–9

This Will Come to an End!

O Lord, sea of love and goodness,
let me not fear too much the storms and
winds of my daily life,
and let me know that there is
ebb and flow
but that the sea remains the sea.

—*Henri Nouwen[1]*

My brethren, count it all joy when ye fall into divers temptations;

Knowing this, that the trying of your faith worketh patience.

But let patience have her perfect work, that ye may be perfect and entire, wanting nothing.

—*James 1:2–4*

Charity suffereth long, and is kind; charity envieth not; charity vaunteth not itself, is not puffed up.

—*1 Corinthians 13:4*

So that we ourselves glory in you in the
churches of God for your patience and faith
in all your persecutions and tribulations
that ye endure:

Which is a manifest token of the
righteous judgment of God, that ye may be
counted worthy of the kingdom of God, for
which ye also suffer.

—*2 Thessalonians 1:4–5*

Thou therefore endure hardness, as a
good soldier of Jesus Christ.

No man that warreth entangleth himself
with the affairs of this life; that he may please
him who hath chosen him to be a soldier.

And if a man also strive for masteries, yet
is he not crowned, except he strive lawfully.

—*2 Timothy 2:3–5*

Therefore being justified by faith, we have
peace with God through our Lord Jesus
Christ:

By whom also we have access by faith
into this grace wherein we stand, and rejoice
in hope of the glory of God.

And not only so, but we glory in tribulations also: knowing that tribulation worketh patience;

And patience, experience; and experience, hope:

And hope maketh not ashamed; because the love of God is shed abroad in our hearts by the Holy Ghost which is given unto us.

—Romans 5:1–5

Rejoicing in hope; patient in tribulation; continuing instant in prayer.

—Romans 12:12

Pray Daily for Deliverance

And there arose a great storm of wind, and the waves beat into the ship, so that it was now full.

And he was in the hinder part of the ship, asleep on a pillow: and they awake him, and say unto him, Master, carest thou not that we perish?

And he arose, and rebuked the wind, and said unto the sea, Peace, be still. And the wind ceased, and there was a great calm.

And he said unto them, Why are ye so fearful? how is it that ye have no faith?

—*Mark 4:37–39*

And, behold, a woman of Canaan came out of the same coasts, and cried unto him, saying, Have mercy on me, O Lord, thou Son of David; my daughter is grievously vexed with a devil.

But he answered her not a word. And his disciples came and besought him, saying, Send her away; for she crieth after us.

But he answered and said, I am not sent but unto the lost sheep of the house of Israel.

Then came she and worshipped him, saying, Lord, help me.

But he answered and said, It is not meet to take the children's bread, and to cast it to dogs.

And she said, Truth, Lord: yet the dogs eat of the crumbs which fall from their masters' table.

Then Jesus answered and said unto her, O woman, great is thy faith: be it unto thee

even as thou wilt. And her daughter was
made whole from that very hour.

—Matthew 15:22–28

O wretched man that I am! who shall
deliver me from the body of this death?

I thank God through Jesus Christ our
Lord. So then with the mind I myself serve
the law of God; but with the flesh the law of
sin.

—Romans 7:24–25

✐ Seek Spiritual Peace

Now the God of hope fill you with all joy
and peace in believing, that ye may abound
in hope, through the power of the Holy
Ghost. . . .

Now the God of peace be with you all.

—Romans 15:13, 33

And the peace of God, which passeth all
understanding, shall keep your hearts and
minds through Christ Jesus.

Finally, brethren, whatsoever things are
true, whatsoever things are honest,
whatsoever things are just, whatsoever

things are pure, whatsoever things are lovely, whatsoever things are of good report; if there be any virtue, and if there be any praise, think on these things.

Those things, which ye have both learned, and received, and heard, and seen in me, do: and the God of peace shall be with you.

—*Philippians 4:7–9*

For a day in thy courts is better than a thousand. I had rather be a doorkeeper in the house of my God, than to dwell in the tents of wickedness.

For the LORD God is a sun and shield: the LORD will give grace and glory: no good thing will he withhold from them that walk uprightly.

O LORD of hosts, blessed is the man that trusteth in thee.

—*Psalm 84:10–12*

Godliness with contentment is great gain.

For we brought nothing into this world, and it is certain we can carry nothing out.

And having food and raiment let us be therewith content.

—*1 Timothy 6:6–8*

—Three—

How Can I Strengthen My Devotional Life?

You've promised so many times to be disciplined, to pray for a certain amount of time each day, to read your Bible "religiously." Now it's time to do these things "graciously." Simply let the Spirit know the desires of your heart each day. He will give you the grace and the will to do the Lord's will, joyfully.

Determine to Live by the Spirit Today!

The real problem of the Christian life comes where people do not usually look for it. It comes the very moment you wake up each morning. All your wishes and hopes for the day rush at you like wild animals. And the first job each morning consists simply in shoving them all back; in listening to that other voice, taking that other point of view, letting that other larger, stronger, quieter life come flowing in. And so on, all day. Standing back from all your natural fussings and frettings; coming in out of the wind.

—C.S. Lewis[1]

If ye then, being evil, know how to give good gifts unto your children: how much more shall your heavenly Father give the Holy Spirit to them that ask him?

—*Luke 11:13*

But when the Comforter is come, whom I will send unto you from the Father, even the

Spirit of truth, which proceedeth from the
Father, he shall testify of me.

—*John 15:26*

Commit to a Life of Obedience

And God spake all these words, saying,

I am the LORD thy God, which have
brought thee out of the land of Egypt, out
of the house of bondage.

Thou shalt have no other gods before me.

Thou shalt not make unto thee any
graven image, or any likeness of any thing
that is in heaven above, or that is in the
earth beneath, or that is in the water under
the earth:

Thou shalt not bow down thyself to
them, nor serve them: for I the LORD thy
God am a jealous God, visiting the iniquity
of the fathers upon the children unto the
third and fourth generation of them that
hate me;

And shewing mercy unto thousands of
them that love me, and keep my
commandments.

Thou shalt not take the name of the LORD thy God in vain; for the LORD will not hold him guiltless that taketh his name in vain.

Remember the sabbath day, to keep it holy.

Six days shalt thou labour, and do all thy work:

But the seventh day is the sabbath of the LORD thy God: in it thou shalt not do any work, thou, nor thy son, nor thy daughter, thy manservant, nor thy maidservant, nor thy cattle, nor thy stranger that is within thy gates:

For in six days the LORD made heaven and earth, the sea, and all that in them is, and rested the seventh day: wherefore the LORD blessed the sabbath day, and hallowed it.

Honour thy father and thy mother: that thy days may be long upon the land which the LORD thy God giveth thee.

Thou shalt not kill.

Thou shalt not commit adultery.

Thou shalt not steal.

Thou shalt not bear false witness against thy neighbour.

Thou shalt not covet thy neighbour's house, thou shalt not covet thy neighbour's wife, nor his manservant, nor his maidservant, nor his ox, nor his ass, nor any thing that is thy neighbour's.

—Exodus 20:1–17

Seeing then that all these things shall be dissolved, what manner of persons ought ye to be in all holy conversation and godliness,

Looking for and hasting unto the coming of the day of God, wherein the heavens being on fire shall be dissolved, and the elements shall melt with fervent heat?

Nevertheless we, according to his promise, look for new heavens and a new earth, wherein dwelleth righteousness.

Wherefore, beloved, seeing that ye look for such things, be diligent that ye may be found of him in peace, without spot, and blameless. . . .

But grow in grace, and in the knowledge of our Lord and Saviour Jesus Christ. To him be glory both now and for ever.

—2 Peter 3:11–14, 18

Be Open to God's Loving Discipline

My son, despise not the chastening of the LORD; neither be weary of his correction:

For whom the LORD loveth he correcteth; even as a father the son in whom he delighteth.

—Proverbs 3:11–12

He, that being often reproved hardeneth his neck, shall suddenly be destroyed, and that without remedy. . . .

A man's pride shall bring him low: but honour shall uphold the humble in spirit.

—Proverbs 29:1, 23

Repent, If Necessary

If my people, which are called by my name, shall humble themselves, and pray, and seek my face, and turn from their wicked ways; then will I hear from heaven, and will forgive their sin, and will heal their land.

—2 Chronicles 7:14

But whoso hearkeneth unto me shall dwell safely, and shall be quiet from fear of evil.

—*Proverbs 1:33*

If so be they will hearken, and turn every man from his evil way, that I may repent me of the evil, which I purpose to do unto them because of the evil of their doings.

—*Jeremiah 26:3*

Repent ye: for the kingdom of heaven is at hand.

—*Matthew 3:2*

Listen to God's Word

My authority in my home is exactly proportional to what I got fresh from God that day. I don't even have to talk about it— there's a heavenly aura when Dads meet God. When I backslide, everything at home falls apart.

—*Robert A. Cook[2]*

Thy word have I hid in mine heart, that I might not sin against thee. . . .

I will delight myself in thy statutes: I will not forget thy word. . . .

So shall I have wherewith to answer him that reproacheth me: for I trust in thy word. . . .

This is my comfort in my affliction: for thy word hath quickened me.

—Psalm 119:11, 16, 42, 50

Thy word is a lamp unto my feet, and a light unto my path.

I have sworn, and I will perform it, that I will keep thy righteous judgments.

I am afflicted very much: quicken me, O LORD, according unto thy word.

Accept, I beseech thee, the freewill offerings of my mouth, O LORD, and teach me thy judgments.

My soul is continually in my hand: yet do I not forget thy law.

The wicked have laid a snare for me: yet I erred not from thy precepts.

—Psalm 119:105–110

All scripture is given by inspiration of God, and is profitable for doctrine, for reproof, for correction, for instruction in righteousness:

That the man of God may be perfect, throughly furnished unto all good works.

—*2 Timothy 3:16–17*

For the word of God is quick, and powerful, and sharper than any twoedged sword, piercing even to the dividing asunder of soul and spirit, and of the joints and marrow, and is a discerner of the thoughts and intents of the heart.

Neither is there any creature that is not manifest in his sight: but all things are naked and opened unto the eyes of him with whom we have to do.

—*Hebrews 4:12–13*

Participate in the Lord's Supper

It was reported of the disciples at Emmaus that they knew Him in the breaking of bread. How did He break the bread? He broke it reverently, thoughtfully, and lovingly.

—E. Paul Hovey[3]

The cup of blessing which we bless, is it not the communion of the blood of Christ? The bread which we break, is it not the communion of the body of Christ?

For we being many are one bread, and one body: for we are all partakers of that one bread. . . .

Whether therefore ye eat, or drink, or whatsoever ye do, do all to the glory of God.

—1 Corinthians 10:16–17, 31

And as they were eating, Jesus took bread, and blessed it, and brake it, and gave it to the disciples, and said, Take, eat; this is my body.

And he took the cup, and gave thanks, and gave it to them, saying, Drink ye all of it;

For this is my blood of the new testament, which is shed for many for the remission of sins.

—Matthew 26:26–28

For I have received of the Lord that which also I delivered unto you, That the Lord Jesus the same night in which he was betrayed took bread:

And when he had given thanks, he brake it, and said, Take, eat: this is my body, which is broken for you: this do in remembrance of me.

After the same manner also he took the cup, when he had supped, saying, This cup is the new testament in my blood: this do ye, as oft as ye drink it, in remembrance of me.

For as often as ye eat this bread, and drink this cup, ye do shew the Lord's death till he come.

Wherefore whosoever shall eat this bread, and drink this cup of the Lord, unworthily, shall be guilty of the body and blood of the Lord.

But let a man examine himself, and so let him eat of that bread, and drink of that cup.

For he that eateth and drinketh unworthily, eateth and drinketh damnation to himself, not discerning the Lord's body.

For this cause many are weak and sickly among you, and many sleep.

For if we would judge ourselves, we should not be judged.

But when we are judged, we are chastened of the Lord, that we should not be condemned with the world.

Wherefore, my brethren, when ye come together to eat, tarry one for another.

—*1 Corinthians 11:23–33*

Tell Others about Christ

A Hindu sent up this comment: "I am not enamored by your dramatic gestures. If you have found Christ, tell us simply and straightforwardly."

I was deeply impressed by his demand that we be simple and straightforward. He was right. The victorious life should and does reduce life to inward unity, and, therefore, to outward simplicity and straightforwardness. We need to be cleansed from all double

*purposes in word and attitude. Our speech
should become "chaste" in the sense of
expressing a single thing.*

—E. Stanley Jones[4]

He first findeth his own brother Simon,
and saith unto him, We have found the
Messias, which is, being interpreted, the
Christ.

And he brought him to Jesus. And when
Jesus beheld him, he said, Thou art Simon
the son of Jona: thou shalt be called Cephas,
which is by interpretation, A stone.

The day following Jesus would go forth
into Galilee, and findeth Philip, and saith
unto him, Follow me.

Now Philip was of Bethsaida, the city of
Andrew and Peter.

Philip findeth Nathanael, and saith unto
him, We have found him, of whom Moses
in the law, and the prophets, did write, Jesus
of Nazareth, the son of Joseph.

And Nathanael said unto him, Can there
any good thing come out of Nazareth?
Philip saith unto him, Come and see.

—John 1:41–46

Four

Why Can't I Find the Time?

"*My* days are hectic, and it's tough to carve out a little alone-time," said Lloyd. "But then when I do, it can be frustrating. I sit with a blank mind, not really knowing what to pray about.

"Then I begin to think: Maybe it's enough, at first, just to be there with the Lord. Maybe that's what fellowship with God is all about."

Set Aside Time for Just Being with God

You can worry that your relationship with
[God] has gone cold,
that you've lost your spiritual edge.
You can think it will take a lot of time, a
month or so of spiritual discipline, to get
going again with him. Then you sit down
and discover, in just minutes, that you don't
have to do a thing—except take some time.
Be alone with him. In what feels like no time
you are caught up again in your love.

—Tim Stafford[1]

Better is an handful with quietness, than
both the hands full with travail and
vexation of spirit.

—*Ecclesiastes 4:6*

Let the words of my mouth, and the
meditation of my heart, be acceptable in thy
sight, O LORD, my strength, and my
redeemer.

—*Psalm 19:14*

I said, I will take heed to my ways, that I sin not with my tongue: I will keep my mouth with a bridle, while the wicked is before me.

I was dumb with silence, I held my peace, even from good; and my sorrow was stirred.

My heart was hot within me, while I was musing the fire burned: then spake I with my tongue.

—Psalm 39:1–3

Hear this, all ye people; give ear, all ye inhabitants of the world:

Both low and high, rich and poor, together.

My mouth shall speak of wisdom; and the meditation of my heart shall be of understanding.

—Psalm 49:1–3

My soul shall be satisfied as with marrow and fatness; and my mouth shall praise thee with joyful lips:

When I remember thee upon my bed, and meditate on thee in the night watches.

—Psalm 63:5–6

And I said, This is my infirmity: but I will remember the years of the right hand of the most High.

I will remember the works of the LORD: surely I will remember thy wonders of old.

I will meditate also of all thy work, and talk of thy doings.

—*Psalm 77:10–12*

Learn to Pray!

If I felt my heart as hard as stone; if I did not love God, or man, or woman, or little child, I would yet say to God in my heart, "O God, see how I trust Thee, because Thou art perfect, and not changeable like me. I do not love Thee, I love nobody. I am not even sorry for it. Thou seest how much I need Thee to come close to me and put Thy arm round me, to say to me, my child: for the worse my state, the greater my need of my Father who loves me. Come to me, and my day will dawn; my love will come back, and, oh!how I

shall love Thee, my God! and know that my
love is Thy love, my blessedness Thy being."

Pray without ceasing.

—1 Thessalonians 5:17

Before they call, I will answer; and while
they are yet speaking, I will hear.

—Isaiah 65:24

And when thou prayest, thou shalt not be
as the hypocrites are: for they love to pray
standing in the synagogues and in the
corners of the streets, that they may be seen
of men. Verily I say unto you, They have
their reward.

But thou, when thou prayest, enter into
thy closet, and when thou hast shut thy
door, pray to thy Father which is in secret;
and thy Father which seeth in secret shall
reward thee openly.

But when ye pray, use not vain
repetitions, as the heathen do: for they think
that they shall be heard for their much
speaking.

Be not ye therefore like unto them: for your Father knoweth what things ye have need of, before ye ask him.

After this manner therefore pray ye: Our Father which art in heaven, Hallowed be thy name.

Thy kingdom come. Thy will be done in earth, as it is in heaven.

Give us this day our daily bread.

And forgive us our debts, as we forgive our debtors.

And lead us not into temptation, but deliver us from evil: For thine is the kingdom, and the power, and the glory, for ever. Amen.

—Matthew 6:5–13

These things have I written unto you that believe on the name of the Son of God; that ye may know that ye have eternal life, and that ye may believe on the name of the Son of God.

And this is the confidence that we have in him, that, if we ask any thing according to his will, he heareth us:

And if we know that he hear us, whatsoever we ask, we know that we have the petitions that we desired of him.

—*1 John 5:13–15*

Ask, and it shall be given you; seek, and ye shall find; knock, and it shall be opened unto you:

For every one that asketh receiveth; and he that seeketh findeth; and to him that knocketh it shall be opened.

Or what man is there of you, whom if his son ask bread, will he give him a stone?

Or if he ask a fish, will he give him a serpent?

If ye then, being evil, know how to give good gifts unto your children, how much more shall your Father which is in heaven give good things to them that ask him?

—*Matthew 7:7–11*

Is any among you afflicted? let him pray. Is any merry? let him sing psalms.

Is any sick among you? let him call for the elders of the church; and let them pray over him, anointing him with oil in the name of the Lord:

And the prayer of faith shall save the sick, and the Lord shall raise him up; and if he have committed sins, they shall be forgiven him.

Confess your faults one to another, and pray one for another, that ye may be healed. The effectual fervent prayer of a righteous man availeth much.

Elias was a man subject to like passions as we are, and he prayed earnestly that it might not rain: and it rained not on the earth by the space of three years and six months.

And he prayed again, and the heaven gave rain, and the earth brought forth her fruit.

—*James 5:13–18*

Let us therefore come boldly unto the throne of grace, that we may obtain mercy, and find grace to help in time of need.

—*Hebrews 4:16*

And whatsoever we ask, we receive of him, because we keep his commandments,

and do those things that are pleasing in his
sight.

—1 John 3:22

Emulate these Biblical Prayer Warriors . . .

*Lift up your heart to him, at the beginning
of every action, somewhat like this: O Jesus,
with all my power I renounce myself, my
own mind, my own will, and my self-love,
and I give myself all to Thee and to Thy
Holy Spirit and Thy divine love. Draw me
out of myself and direct me in this action
according to Thy holy will.*

—Jean Eudes[3]

Let us draw near with a true heart in full
assurance of faith, having our hearts
sprinkled from an evil conscience, and our
bodies washed with pure water.

—Hebrews 10:22

Elijah

And Elijah said unto all the people, Come near unto me. And all the people came near unto him. And he repaired the altar of the LORD that was broken down.

And Elijah took twelve stones, according to the number of the tribes of the sons of Jacob, unto whom the word of the LORD came, saying, Israel shall be thy name:

And with the stones he built an altar in the name of the LORD: and he made a trench about the altar, as great as would contain two measures of seed.

And he put the wood in order, and cut the bullock in pieces, and laid him on the wood, and said, Fill four barrels with water, and pour it on the burnt sacrifice, and on the wood.

And he said, Do it the second time. And they did it the second time. And he said, Do it the third time. And they did it the third time.

And the water ran round about the altar; and he filled the trench also with water.

And it came to pass at the time of the offering of the evening sacrifice, that Elijah the prophet came near, and said, LORD God of Abraham, Isaac, and of Israel, let it be known this day that thou art God in Israel, and that I am thy servant, and that I have done all these things at thy word.

Hear me, O LORD, hear me, that this people may know that thou art the LORD God, and that thou hast turned their heart back again.

Then the fire of the LORD fell, and consumed the burnt sacrifice, and the wood, and the stones, and the dust, and licked up the water that was in the trench.

And when all the people saw it, they fell on their faces: and they said, The LORD, he is the God; the LORD, he is the God.

—1 Kings 18:30–39

✒Abraham

And Abraham drew near, and said, Wilt thou also destroy the righteous with the wicked?

Peradventure there be fifty righteous within the city: wilt thou also destroy and not spare the place for the fifty righteous that are therein?

That be far from thee to do after this manner, to slay the righteous with the wicked: and that the righteous should be as the wicked, that be far from thee: Shall not the Judge of all the earth do right?

And the LORD said, If I find in Sodom fifty righteous within the city, then I will spare all the place for their sakes.

And Abraham answered and said, Behold now, I have taken upon me to speak unto the Lord, which am but dust and ashes:

Peradventure there shall lack five of the fifty righteous: wilt thou destroy all the city for lack of five? And he said, If I find there forty and five, I will not destroy it.

And he spake unto him yet again, and said, Peradventure there shall be forty found there. And he said, I will not do it for forty's sake.

And he said unto him, Oh let not the Lord be angry, and I will speak: Peradventure there shall thirty be found there. And he said, I will not do it, if I find thirty there.

And he said, Behold now, I have taken upon me to speak unto the Lord: Peradventure there shall be twenty found there. And he said, I will not destroy it for twenty's sake.

And he said, Oh let not the Lord be angry, and I will speak yet but this once: Peradventure ten shall be found there. And he said, I will not destroy it for ten's sake.

—*Genesis 18:23–32*

✐*Moses*

And Moses cried unto the LORD, saying, Heal her now, O God, I beseech thee.

And the LORD said unto Moses, If her father had but spit in her face, should she not be ashamed seven days? let her be shut out from the camp seven days, and after that let her be received in again.

And Miriam was shut out from the camp seven days: and the people journeyed not till Miriam was brought in again.

—*Numbers 12:13–15*

# Gideon

And Gideon said unto God, If thou wilt save Israel by mine hand, as thou hast said,

Behold, I will put a fleece of wool in the floor; and if the dew be on the fleece only, and it be dry upon all the earth beside, then shall I know that thou wilt save Israel by mine hand, as thou hast said.

And it was so: for he rose up early on the morrow, and thrust the fleece together, and wringed the dew out of the fleece, a bowl full of water.

And Gideon said unto God, Let not thine anger be hot against me, and I will speak but this once: let me prove, I pray thee, but this once with the fleece; let it now be dry only upon the fleece, and upon all the ground let there be dew.

And God did so that night: for it was dry upon the fleece only, and there was dew on all the ground.

—Judges 6:36–40

 # Jacob

And Jacob said, O God of my father Abraham, and God of my father Isaac, the LORD which saidst unto me, Return unto thy country, and to thy kindred, and I will deal well with thee:

I am not worthy of the least of all the mercies, and of all the truth, which thou hast shewed unto thy servant; for with my staff I passed over this Jordan; and now I am become two bands.

Deliver me, I pray thee, from the hand of my brother, from the hand of Esau: for I fear him, lest he will come and smite me, and the mother with the children.

And thou saidst, I will surely do thee good, and make thy seed as the sand of the sea, which cannot be numbered for multitude.

—Genesis 32:9–12

Solomon

In Gibeon the LORD appeared to Solomon in a dream by night: and God said, Ask what I shall give thee.

And Solomon said, Thou hast shewed unto thy servant David my father great mercy, according as he walked before thee in truth, and in righteousness, and in uprightness of heart with thee; and thou hast kept for him this great kindness, that thou hast given him a son to sit on his throne, as it is this day.

And now, O LORD my God, thou hast made thy servant king instead of David my father: and I am but a little child: I know not how to go out or come in.

And thy servant is in the midst of thy people which thou hast chosen, a great people, that cannot be numbered nor counted for multitude.

Give therefore thy servant an understanding heart to judge thy people, that I may discern between good and bad:

for who is able to judge this thy so great a people?

And the speech pleased the Lord, that Solomon had asked this thing.

And God said unto him, Because thou hast asked this thing, and hast not asked for thyself long life; neither hast asked riches for thyself, nor hast asked the life of thine enemies; but hast asked for thyself understanding to discern judgment;

Behold, I have done according to thy words: lo, I have given thee a wise and an understanding heart; so that there was none like thee before thee, neither after thee shall any arise like unto thee.

And I have also given thee that which thou hast not asked, both riches, and honour: so that there shall not be any among the kings like unto thee all thy days.

—*1 Kings 3:5–13*

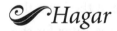 ## Hagar

And the angel of the LORD found her by a fountain of water in the wilderness, by the fountain in the way to Shur.

And he said, Hagar, Sarai's maid, whence camest thou? and whither wilt thou go? And she said, I flee from the face of my mistress Sarai.

And the angel of the LORD said unto her, Return to thy mistress, and submit thyself under her hands.

And the angel of the LORD said unto her, I will multiply thy seed exceedingly, that it shall not be numbered for multitude.

And the angel of the LORD said unto her, Behold, thou art with child, and shalt bear a son, and shalt call his name Ishmael; because the LORD hath heard thy affliction.

And he will be a wild man; his hand will be against every man, and every man's hand against him; and he shall dwell in the presence of all his brethren.

And she called the name of the LORD that spake unto her, Thou God seest me: for she said, Have I also here looked after him that seeth me?

—*Genesis 16:7–13*

Samson

And Samson called unto the LORD, and said, O Lord GOD, remember me, I pray thee, and strengthen me, I pray thee, only this once, O God, that I may be at once avenged of the Philistines for my two eyes.

And Samson took hold of the two middle pillars upon which the house stood, and on which it was borne up, of the one with his right hand, and of the other with his left.

And Samson said, Let me die with the Philistines. And he bowed himself with all his might; and the house fell upon the lords, and upon all the people that were therein. So the dead which he slew at his death were more than they which he slew in his life.

—Judges 16:28–30

David

And David inquired of the LORD, saying, Shall I go up to the Philistines? wilt thou deliver them into mine hand? And the LORD said unto David, Go up: for I will doubtless deliver the Philistines into thine hand.

And David came to Baal-perazim, and David smote them there, and said, The LORD hath broken forth upon mine enemies before me, as the breach of waters. Therefore he called the name of that place Baal-perazim.

And there they left their images, and David and his men burned them.

And the Philistines came up yet again, and spread themselves in the valley of Rephaim.

And when David enquired of the LORD, he said, Thou shalt not go up; but fetch a compass behind them, and come upon them over against the mulberry trees.

And let it be, when thou hearest the sound of a going in the tops of the mulberry trees, that then thou shalt bestir thyself: for then shall the LORD go out before thee, to smite the host of the Philistines.

And David did so, as the LORD had commanded him; and smote the Philistines from Geba until thou come to Gazer.

—*2 Samuel 5:19–25*

✒ Hezekiah

In those days was Hezekiah sick unto death. And the prophet Isaiah the son of Amoz came to him, and said unto him, Thus saith the LORD, Set thine house in order; for thou shalt die, and not live.

Then he turned his face to the wall, and prayed unto the LORD, saying,

I beseech thee, O LORD, remember now how I have walked before thee in truth and with a perfect heart, and have done that which is good in thy sight. And Hezekiah wept sore.

And it came to pass, afore Isaiah was gone out into the middle court, that the word of the LORD came to him, saying,

Turn again, and tell Hezekiah the captain of my people, Thus saith the LORD, the God of David thy father, I have heard thy prayer, I have seen thy tears: behold, I will heal thee: on the third day thou shalt go up unto the house of the LORD.

And I will add unto thy days fifteen years; and I will deliver thee and this city out of the hand of the king of Assyria; and I will defend this city for mine own sake, and for my servant David's sake.

And Isaiah said, Take a lump of figs. And they took and laid it on the boil, and he recovered.

And Hezekiah said unto Isaiah, What shall be the sign that the LORD will heal me, and that I shall go up into the house of the LORD the third day?

And Isaiah said, This sign shalt thou have of the LORD, that the LORD will do the thing that he hath spoken: shall the shadow go forward ten degrees, or go back ten degrees?

And Hezekiah answered, It is a light thing for the shadow to go down ten degrees: nay, but let the shadow return backward ten degrees.

And Isaiah the prophet cried unto the LORD: and he brought the shadow ten degrees backward, by which it had gone down in the dial of Ahaz.

—2 Kings 20:1–11

Elijah

And it came to pass at the time of the offering of the evening sacrifice, that Elijah the prophet came near, and said, LORD God of Abraham, Isaac, and of Israel, let it be known this day that thou art God in Israel, and that I am thy servant, and that I have done all these things at thy word.

Hear me, O LORD, hear me, that this people may know that thou art the LORD God, and that thou hast turned their heart back again.

Then the fire of the LORD fell, and consumed the burnt sacrifice, and the wood, and the stones, and the dust, and licked up the water that was in the trench.

—1 Kings 18:36–38

Elisha

And Elisha prayed, and said, LORD, I pray thee, open his eyes, that he may see. And the LORD opened the eyes of the young man; and he saw: and, behold, the mountain was full of horses and chariots of fire round about Elisha.

And when they came down to him, Elisha prayed unto the LORD, and said, Smite this people, I pray thee, with blindness. And he smote them with blindness according to the word of Elisha.

And Elisha said unto them, This is not the way, neither is this the city: follow me, and I will bring you to the man whom ye seek. But he led them to Samaria.

And it came to pass, when they were come into Samaria, that Elisha said, LORD, open the eyes of these men, that they may see. And the LORD opened their eyes, and they saw; and, behold, they were in the midst of Samaria.

—2 Kings 6:17–20

Daniel

Then was the secret revealed unto Daniel in a night vision. Then Daniel blessed the God of heaven.

Daniel answered and said, Blessed be the name of God for ever and ever: for wisdom and might are his:

And he changeth the times and the seasons: he removeth kings, and setteth up kings: he giveth wisdom unto the wise, and knowledge to them that know understanding:

He revealeth the deep and secret things: he knoweth what is in the darkness, and the light dwelleth with him.

I thank thee, and praise thee, O thou God of my fathers, who hast given me wisdom and might, and hast made known unto me now what we desired of thee: for thou hast now made known unto us the king's matter.

—*Daniel 2:19–23*

And whiles I was speaking, and praying, and confessing my sin and the sin of my people Israel, and presenting my supplication before the LORD my God for the holy mountain of my God;

Yea, whiles I was speaking in prayer, even the man Gabriel, whom I had seen in the vision at the beginning, being caused to fly swiftly, touched me about the time of the evening oblation.

And he informed me, and talked with me, and said, O Daniel, I am now come forth to give thee skill and understanding.

At the beginning of thy supplications the commandment came forth, and I am come to shew thee; for thou art greatly beloved: therefore understand the matter, and consider the vision.

—*Daniel 9:20–23*

❧ Jesus

And he went a little farther, and fell on his face, and prayed, saying, O my Father, if it be possible, let this cup pass from me: nevertheless not as I will, but as thou wilt.

And he cometh unto the disciples, and findeth them asleep, and saith unto Peter, What, could ye not watch with me one hour?

Watch and pray, that ye enter not into temptation: the spirit indeed is willing, but the flesh is weak.

He went away again the second time, and prayed, saying, O my Father, if this cup may not pass away from me, except I drink it, thy will be done.

And he came and found them asleep again: for their eyes were heavy.

And he left them, and went away again, and prayed the third time, saying the same words.

—*Matthew 26:39–44*

Paul

Wherefore I desire that ye faint not at my tribulations for you, which is your glory.

For this cause I bow my knees unto the Father of our Lord Jesus Christ,

Of whom the whole family in heaven and earth is named,

That he would grant you, according to the riches of his glory, to be strengthened with might by his Spirit in the inner man;

That Christ may dwell in your hearts by faith; that ye, being rooted and grounded in love,

May be able to comprehend with all saints what is the breadth, and length, and depth, and height;

And to know the love of Christ, which passeth knowledge, that ye might be filled with all the fulness of God.

Now unto him that is able to do exceeding abundantly above all that we ask or think, according to the power that worketh in us,

Unto him be glory in the church by Christ Jesus throughout all ages, world without end. Amen.

—*Ephesians 3:13–21*

Remember: Even Your Time Is In God's Hands

Set no time to the Lord, the creator of time, for His time is always best.

—*Samuel Rutherford*

But, beloved, be not ignorant of this one thing, that one day is with the Lord as a thousand years, and a thousand years as one day.

—*2 Peter 3:8*

And he said unto me, My grace is sufficient for thee: for my strength is made perfect in weakness. Most gladly therefore will I rather glory in my infirmities, that the power of Christ may rest upon me.

Therefore I take pleasure in infirmities, in reproaches, in necessities, in persecutions, in distresses for Christ's sake: for when I am weak, then am I strong.

—*2 Corinthians 12:9–10*

And let us not be weary in well doing: for in due season we shall reap, if we faint not.

—*Galatians 6:9*

Thou wilt keep him in perfect peace, whose mind is stayed on thee: because he trusteth in thee.

—*Isaiah 26:3*

Truly my soul waiteth upon God: from him cometh my salvation.

He only is my rock and my salvation; he
is my defence; I shall not be greatly moved.

—*Psalm 62:1–2*

I waited patiently for the LORD; and he
inclined unto me, and heard my cry.

He brought me up also out of an horrible
pit, out of the miry clay, and set my feet
upon a rock, and established my goings.

And he hath put a new song in my
mouth, even praise unto our God: many
shall see it, and fear, and shall trust in the
LORD.

—*Psalm 40:1–3*

So . . . Make Good Use of Your Time

*The great thing, if one can, is to stop
regarding all the unpleasant things as
interruptions of one's "own," or "real" life.
The truth is of course that what one calls the
interruptions are precisely one's real life—
the life God is sending one day by day.*

—*C. S. Lewis*[4]

Now it is high time to awake out of sleep: for now is our salvation nearer than when we believed.

—*Romans 13:11*

To every thing there is a season, and a time to every purpose under the heaven:
A time to be born, and a time to die; a time to plant, and a time to pluck up that which is planted;
A time to kill, and a time to heal; a time to break down, and a time to build up;
A time to weep, and a time to laugh; a time to mourn, and a time to dance;
A time to cast away stones, and a time to gather stones together; a time to embrace, and a time to refrain from embracing;
A time to get, and a time to lose; a time to keep, and a time to cast away;
A time to rend, and a time to sew; a time to keep silence, and a time to speak;
A time to love, and a time to hate; a time of war, and a time of peace.

—*Ecclesiastes 3:1–8*

[Redeem] the time, because the days are evil.

—*Ephesians 5:16*

Five

How Should I Approach My Work?

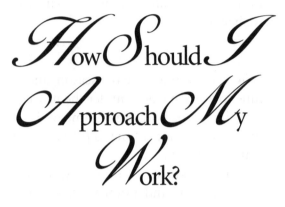

Have you ever fantasized about just taking off—heading away from the daily grind of responsibilities, taking the next train out of town? It's not that easy, of course. Our problems have a way of following us around, no matter how much we might try to hide.

The better way is to face life head-on, with all it's trying circumstances. It's especially true when it comes to our work, because there we can easily get bored, frustrated, and angry. But the Lord cares about our work. In fact, He invented it and wants us to find a significant level of satisfaction in it.

Is the Daily Grind Getting You Down?

The reason I resigned at this time is because the duties and the pressures of this position have begun to make me into something that I don't want to be.

—Dan Issel, former head coach of the Denver Nuggets[1]

The LORD God sent him forth from the garden of Eden, to till the ground from whence he was taken.

—Genesis 3:23

What profit hath a man of all his labour
which he taketh under the sun?

—*Ecclesiastes 1:3*

❧Have You Lost the Joy of Honest Work?

I saw under the sun the place of
judgment, that wickedness was there; and
the place of righteousness, that iniquity was
there.

I said in mine heart, God shall judge the
righteous and the wicked: for there is a time
there for every purpose and for every work.

I said in mine heart concerning the estate
of the sons of men, that God might
manifest them, and that they might see that
they themselves are beasts.

For that which befalleth the sons of men
befalleth beasts; even one thing befalleth
them: as the one dieth, so dieth the other;
yea, they have all one breath; so that a man
hath no preeminence above a beast: for all is
vanity.

All go unto one place; all are of the dust,
and all turn to dust again.

Who knoweth the spirit of man that
goeth upward, and the spirit of the beast
that goeth downward to the earth?

—*Ecclesiastes 3:16–21*

❧ Are You Wondering: "What's the Point?"

Go thy way, eat thy bread with joy, and
drink thy wine with a merry heart; for God
now accepteth thy works.

Let thy garments be always white; and let
thy head lack no ointment.

Live joyfully with the wife whom thou
lovest all the days of the life of thy vanity,
which he hath given thee under the sun, all
the days of thy vanity: for that is thy portion
in this life, and in thy labour which thou
takest under the sun.

Whatsoever thy hand findeth to do, do it
with thy might; for there is no work, nor
device, nor knowledge, nor wisdom, in the
grave, whither thou goest.

—*Ecclesiastes 9:7–10*

The LORD is my shepherd; I shall not want.

He maketh me to lie down in green pastures: he leadeth me beside the still waters.

—Psalm 23:1–2

Remember: You Have a Purpose Here on Earth!

This is the longing of all mankind—to have security, to know where one's place is. God created man and then he created a place for him, the Garden of Eden. When man lost God, he lost at the same time his place. Since then, the longing for a place where he belongs, where he feels at home, is in the heart of every human being. In light of this, Jesus' promise "to prepare a place" for us is filled with new meaning. Those who have found him have found their place.

—Walter Trobisch[2]

Let us hear the conclusion of the whole matter: Fear God, and keep his commandments: for this is the whole duty of man.

For God shall bring every work into judgment, with every secret thing, whether it be good, or whether it be evil.

—*Ecclesiastes 12:13–14*

For now we see through a glass, darkly; but then face to face: now I know in part; but then shall I know even as also I am known.

And now abideth faith, hope, charity, these three; but the greatest of these is charity.

—*1 Corinthians 13:12–13*

Let not your heart be troubled: ye believe in God, believe also in me.

In my Father's house are many mansions: if it were not so, I would have told you. I go to prepare a place for you.

And if I go and prepare a place for you, I will come again, and receive you unto myself; that where I am, there ye may be also.

And whither I go ye know, and the way ye know.

—John 14:1–4

There remaineth therefore a rest to the people of God.

—Hebrews 4:9

Yes, God Holds Your Future

And I saw a new heaven and a new earth: for the first heaven and the first earth were passed away; and there was no more sea.

And I John saw the holy city, new Jerusalem, coming down from God out of heaven, prepared as a bride adorned for her husband.

And I heard a great voice out of heaven saying, Behold, the tabernacle of God is with men, and he will dwell with them, and they shall be his people, and God himself shall be with them, and be their God.

And God shall wipe away all tears from their eyes; and there shall be no more death, neither sorrow, nor crying, neither shall there be any more pain: for the former things are passed away.

And he that sat upon the throne said, Behold, I make all things new. And he said unto me, Write: for these words are true and faithful.

—Revelation 21:1–5

So Enjoy the Life He Has Given You

In every thing give thanks: for this is the will of God in Christ Jesus concerning you.

—1 Thessalonians 5:18

Thou hast turned for me my mourning into dancing: thou hast put off my sackcloth, and girded me with gladness;

To the end that my glory may sing praise to thee, and not be silent. O LORD my God, I will give thanks unto thee for ever.

—Psalm 30:11–12

They that sow in tears shall reap in joy.

He that goeth forth and weepeth, bearing precious seed, shall doubtless come again with rejoicing, bringing his sheaves with him.

—Psalm 126:5–6

But rejoice, inasmuch as ye are partakers of Christ's sufferings; that, when his glory shall be revealed, ye may be glad also with exceeding joy.

—1 Peter 4:13

—Six—

Suppose I'm a Family Man?

Life in the family can be simply wonderful. Or it can be a crazy, mixed-up jumble of competing egos and unrealistic demands. How's it going in your family? If you're looking for some guidance, the Bible is a great place to turn!

109

When You're Irritable at Home . . .

Women, with your help and understanding, we guys can do better. And we will do better. We will, inch by painful inch, overcome our natural handicaps, and we will rise to meet your standards for personal behavior. It will not happen tomorrow, or the next day, or the day after that, or even necessarily before the earth crashes back into the sun. But it will happen, because we guys are sick and tired of not living up to your expectations, and we are . . . really going to start trying to change. But not until after the playoffs.

—*Dave Barry[1]*

Why is thy countenance sad, seeing thou art not sick?

—*Nehemiah 2:2*

A merry heart doeth good like a medicine: but a broken spirit drieth the bones.

—*Proverbs 17:22*

I called upon the LORD in distress: the LORD answered me, and set me in a large place.

The LORD is on my side; I will not fear: what can man do unto me?

The LORD taketh my part with them that help me: therefore shall I see my desire upon them that hate me.

It is better to trust in the LORD than to put confidence in man.

It is better to trust in the LORD than to put confidence in princes.

—*Psalm 118:5–9*

Work at Strengthening Your Marriage . . .

How do I love thee? Let me count the ways.

I love thee to the depth and breadth and height

My soul can reach, when feeling out of sight

For the ends of Being and ideal Grace.

I love thee to the level of every day's

Most quiet need, by sun and candle-light.

I love thee freely, as men strive for Right;

I love thee purely, as they turn from Praise.

I love thee with the passion put to use

In my old griefs, and with my childhood's faith.

I love thee with a love I seemed to lose

With my lost saints,—I love thee with the breath,

Smiles, tears, of all my life!—and, if God choose,

I shall but love thee better after death.

—Elizabeth Barrett Browning

So ought men to love their wives as their own bodies.

—*Ephesians 5:28*

Submitting yourselves one to another in the fear of God.

—*Ephesians 5:21*

Let thy fountain be blessed: and rejoice with the wife of thy youth.

Let her be as the loving hind and pleasant roe; let her breasts satisfy thee at all times; and be thou ravished always with her love.

And why wilt thou, my son, be ravished with a strange woman, and embrace the bosom of a stranger?

—*Proverbs 5:18–20*

Live joyfully with the wife whom thou lovest all the days of the life of thy vanity, which he hath given thee under the sun, all the days of thy vanity: for that is thy portion in this life, and in thy labour which thou takest under the sun.

—*Ecclesiastes 9:9*

Ye husbands, dwell with them according to knowledge, giving honour unto the wife, as unto the weaker vessel, and as being heirs together of the grace of life; that your prayers be not hindered.

—*1 Peter 3:7*

Marriage is honourable in all, and the bed undefiled.

—*Hebrews 13:4*

Help Your Children to Follow the Lord

Each of us can change our own little world. Fathers who are honest with themselves will admit that we all make mistakes. We have all made bad decisions. Some of those decisions have to be reversed. If you have accepted a promotion and a transfer that takes you a step up the corporate ladder at the expense of your kids, maybe you need to think about taking a step back. More important than providing a life of ease for your kids is making sure they know you love them unconditionally.

—Mike Singletary[2]

Train up a child in the way he should go: and when he is old, he will not depart from it.

—Proverbs 22:6

Only take heed to thyself, and keep thy soul diligently, lest thou forget the things which thine eyes have seen, and lest they depart from thy heart all the days of thy life: but teach them thy sons, and thy sons' sons;

Specially the day that thou stoodest before the LORD thy God in Horeb, when the LORD said unto me, Gather me the people together, and I will make them hear my words, that they may learn to fear me all the days that they shall live upon the earth, and that they may teach their children.

—Deuteronomy 4:9–10

And these words, which I command thee this day, shall be in thine heart:

And thou shalt teach them diligently unto thy children, and shalt talk of them when thou sittest in thine house, and when thou walkest by the way, and when thou liest down, and when thou risest up.

And thou shalt bind them for a sign upon thine hand, and they shall be as frontlets between thine eyes.

And thou shalt write them upon the posts of thy house, and on thy gates.

—Deuteronomy 6:6–9

Ye fathers, provoke not your children to wrath: but bring them up in the nurture and admonition of the Lord.

—*Ephesians 6:4*

✒Let Children Know How Much God Loves Them

At the same time came the disciples unto Jesus, saying, Who is the greatest in the kingdom of heaven?

And Jesus called a little child unto him, and set him in the midst of them,

And said, Verily I say unto you, Except ye be converted, and become as little children, ye shall not enter into the kingdom of heaven.

Whosoever therefore shall humble himself as this little child, the same is greatest in the kingdom of heaven.

And whoso shall receive one such little child in my name receiveth me.

But whoso shall offend one of these little ones which believe in me, it were better for him that a millstone were hanged about his neck, and that he were drowned in the depth of the sea.

Woe unto the world because of offences! for it must needs be that offences come; but woe to that man by whom the offence cometh!

Wherefore if thy hand or thy foot offend thee, cut them off, and cast them from thee: it is better for thee to enter into life halt or maimed, rather than having two hands or two feet to be cast into everlasting fire.

And if thine eye offend thee, pluck it out, and cast it from thee: it is better for thee to enter into life with one eye, rather than having two eyes to be cast into hell fire.

Take heed that ye despise not one of these little ones; for I say unto you, That in heaven their angels do always behold the face of my Father which is in heaven.

—Matthew 18:1–10

Provide Loving Discipline at Home

Children, obey your parents in all things: for this is well pleasing unto the Lord.

—Colossians 3:20

Withhold not correction from the child:
for if thou beatest him with the rod, he shall
not die.

—Proverbs 23:13

Correct thy son, and he shall give thee
rest; yea, he shall give delight unto thy soul.

—Proverbs 29:17

Now no chastening for the present
seemeth to be joyous, but grievous:
nevertheless afterward it yieldeth the
peaceable fruit of righteousness unto them
which are exercised thereby.

—Hebrews 12:11

He that spareth his rod hateth his son:
but he that loveth him chasteneth him
betimes.

—Proverbs 13:24

Learn to Work Together As a Family

Bear ye one another's burdens, and so
fulfil the law of Christ.

For if a man think himself to be something, when he is nothing, he deceiveth himself.

But let every man prove his own work, and then shall he have rejoicing in himself alone, and not in another.

—*Galatians 6:2–4*

With all lowliness and meekness, with longsuffering, forbearing one another in love;

Endeavouring to keep the unity of the Spirit in the bond of peace.

—*Ephesians 4:2–3*

Worship God Together Every Sunday

Not forsaking the assembling of ourselves together, as the manner of some is; but exhorting one another: and so much the more, as ye see the day approaching.

—*Hebrews 10:25*

Could I Improve My Witness?

You say you are a Christian. Does anyone else know it? Your family members and closest friends probably know about your faith in Christ. But are you ready to spread the word? It's time to find out more about what that involves, so read on.

Are You Willing to Speak Up for Christ?

*The really important thing is that in those
early days the pagans saw in Christianity
and in the Church a power that could cope
with and mend the human situation. They
saw in Christianity a power which they did
not possess—and they wanted it. It will
always be true that the outsider will have no
use for an alleged faith which is
demonstrably ineffective. Long ago
Nietzsche, the atheist philosopher, issued the
challenge: "Show me that you are redeemed
and then I will believe in your Redeemer."*

—William Barclay[1]

Jesus came and spake unto them, saying,
All power is given unto me in heaven and in
earth.

Go ye therefore, and teach all nations,
baptizing them in the name of the Father,
and of the Son, and of the Holy Ghost:

Teaching them to observe all things
whatsoever I have commanded you: and, lo,

I am with you alway, even unto the end of the world.

—Matthew 28:18–20

Preach the word; be instant in season, out of season; reprove, rebuke, exhort with all longsuffering and doctrine.

—2 Timothy 4:2

Whosoever shall confess me before men, him shall the Son of man also confess before the angels of God:

But he that denieth me before men shall be denied before the angels of God.

—Luke 12:8–9

Does Your Lifestyle Convey Your Faith?

Any time you commit to living a more godly life, you are entering enemy territory. Expect spiritual conflict. Whether it is fashionable or not, integrity involves a price, but the cost pales in comparison with the cost of

compromise. People can ruin your
reputation, but no one can
take away your integrity.

—*Paul Kroger*[2]

As ye have therefore received Christ Jesus the Lord, so walk ye in him.

—*Colossians 2:6*

Ye are the light of the world. A city that is set on an hill cannot be hid.

Neither do men light a candle, and put it under a bushel, but on a candlestick; and it giveth light unto all that are in the house.

Let your light so shine before men, that they may see your good works, and glorify your Father which is in heaven.

—*Matthew 5:14–16*

The night is far spent, the day is at hand: let us therefore cast off the works of darkness, and let us put on the armour of light.

Let us walk honestly, as in the day; not in rioting and drunkenness, not in chambering and wantonness, not in strife and envying.

But put ye on the Lord Jesus Christ, and make not provision for the flesh, to fulfil the lusts thereof.

—*Romans 13:12–14*

✒ *Staying Focused on God's Will?*

Let the words of my mouth, and the meditation of my heart, be acceptable in thy sight, O LORD, my strength, and my redeemer.

—*Psalm 19:14*

Blessed are the undefiled in the way, who walk in the law of the LORD.

Blessed are they that keep his testimonies, and that seek him with the whole heart.

They also do no iniquity: they walk in his ways.

Thou hast commanded us to keep thy precepts diligently.

O that my ways were directed to keep thy statutes!

—*Psalm 119:1–5*

No man can serve two masters: for either he will hate the one, and love the other; or else he will hold to the one, and despise the other. Ye cannot serve God and mammon.

—*Matthew 6:24*

ᝌRemaining Accountable and Responsibile?

They that are Christ's have crucified the flesh with the affections and lusts.

—*Galatians 5:24*

For the grace of God that bringeth salvation hath appeared to all men,
Teaching us that, denying ungodliness and worldly lusts, we should live soberly, righteously, and godly, in this present world.

—*Titus 2:11–12*

ᝌBeing Kind to All?

And, behold, a certain lawyer stood up, and tempted him, saying, Master, what shall I do to inherit eternal life?

He said unto him, What is written in the law? how readest thou?

And he answering said, Thou shalt love the Lord thy God with all thy heart, and with all thy soul, and with all thy strength, and with all thy mind; and thy neighbour as thyself.

And he said unto him, Thou hast answered right: this do, and thou shalt live.

But he, willing to justify himself, said unto Jesus, And who is my neighbour?

And Jesus answering said, A certain man went down from Jerusalem to Jericho, and fell among thieves, which stripped him of his raiment, and wounded him, and departed, leaving him half dead.

And by chance there came down a certain priest that way: and when he saw him, he passed by on the other side.

And likewise a Levite, when he was at the place, came and looked on him, and passed by on the other side.

But a certain Samaritan, as he journeyed, came where he was: and when he saw him, he had compassion on him,

And went to him, and bound up his wounds, pouring in oil and wine, and set him on his own beast, and brought him to an inn, and took care of him.

And on the morrow when he departed, he took out two pence, and gave them to the host, and said unto him, Take care of him; and whatsoever thou spendest more, when I come again, I will repay thee.

Which now of these three, thinkest thou, was neighbour unto him that fell among the thieves?

And he said, He that shewed mercy on him. Then said Jesus unto him, Go, and do thou likewise.

—*Luke 10:25–37*

Maintaining a Strong Faith?

Now faith is the substance of things hoped for, the evidence of things not seen.

—*Hebrews 11:1*

Verily I say unto you, If ye have faith as a grain of mustard seed, ye shall say unto this mountain, Remove hence to yonder place; and it shall remove; and nothing shall be impossible unto you.

—Matthew 17:20

Displaying Perseverance?

By much slothfulness the building decayeth; and through idleness of the hands the house droppeth through.

—Ecclesiastes 10:18

Wherefore seeing we also are compassed about with so great a cloud of witnesses, let us lay aside every weight, and the sin which doth so easily beset us, and let us run with patience the race that is set before us,

Looking unto Jesus the author and finisher of our faith; who for the joy that was set before him endured the cross, despising the shame, and is set down at the right hand of the throne of God.

For consider him that endured such contradiction of sinners against himself, lest ye be wearied and faint in your minds.

Ye have not yet resisted unto blood, striving against sin.

—Hebrews 12:1–4

Although the fig tree shall not blossom, neither shall fruit be in the vines; the labour of the olive shall fail, and the fields shall yield no meat; the flock shall be cut off from the fold, and there shall be no herd in the stalls:

Yet I will rejoice in the LORD, I will joy in the God of my salvation.

The LORD God is my strength, and he will make my feet like hinds' feet, and he will make me to walk upon mine high places.

—Habakkuk 3:17–19

Showing Hospitality toward Others?

He that receiveth a prophet in the name of a prophet shall receive a prophet's reward; and he that receiveth a righteous man in the name of a righteous man shall receive a righteous man's reward.

And whosoever shall give to drink unto one of these little ones a cup of cold water only in the name of a disciple, verily I say unto you, he shall in no wise lose his reward.

—*Matthew 10:41–42*

❧*Living with Appropriate Humility?*

God resisteth the proud, but giveth grace unto the humble.

—*James 4:6*

Humble yourselves therefore under the mighty hand of God, that he may exalt you in due time.

—*1 Peter 5:6*

Two men went up into the temple to pray; the one a Pharisee, and the other a publican.

The Pharisee stood and prayed thus with himself, God, I thank thee, that I am not as other men are, extortioners, unjust, adulterers, or even as this publican.

I fast twice in the week, I give tithes of all that I possess.

And the publican, standing afar off, would not lift up so much as his eyes unto heaven, but smote upon his breast, saying, God be merciful to me a sinner.

I tell you, this man went down to his house justified rather than the other: for every one that exalteth himself shall be abased; and he that humbleth himself shall be exalted.

—*Luke 18:10–14*

The fear of the LORD is the instruction of wisdom; and before honour is humility.

—*Proverbs 15:33*

—Eight—

What Can I Do for the Lord?

Every believer is given spiritual gifts to be used in building up the body of Christ. We do it by serving one another in the church, with the skills and abilities that God gave us. We don't do spiritual work unless we are relying on the gifts and the empowerment of the Spirit Himself. Approaching it any other way, we may produce a showy display of self-sacrifice or apparent success. But the accomplishments

will be hollow, indeed, and the results won't stand for eternity.

God Calls You to Service

Why would a loving God put His children to work as soon as He created them? Because He knew human labor was a blessing. He knew it would provide them challenges, excitement, adventure, and rewards that nothing else would. He knew that creatures made in His image needed to devote their time to meaningful tasks.

—*Bill Hybels*[1]

For we are his workmanship, created in Christ Jesus unto good works, which God hath before ordained that we should walk in them.

—*Ephesians 2:10*

For to me to live is Christ, and to die is gain.

—*Philippians 1:21*

You Have the Spiritual Gifts to Do It!

Spiritual gifts are God's way of administering His grace to others. When we exercise our gifts, we function as the hands and feet of Christ.

—Charles Stanley

As every man hath received the gift, even so minister the same one to another, as good stewards of the manifold grace of God.

If any man speak, let him speak as the oracles of God; if any man minister, let him do it as of the ability which God giveth: that God in all things may be glorified through Jesus Christ, to whom be praise and dominion for ever and ever.

—1 Peter 4:10–11

Now concerning spiritual gifts, brethren, I would not have you ignorant.

Ye know that ye were Gentiles, carried away unto these dumb idols, even as ye were led.

Wherefore I give you to understand, that no man speaking by the Spirit of God calleth Jesus accursed: and that no man can say that Jesus is the Lord, but by the Holy Ghost.

Now there are diversities of gifts, but the same Spirit.

And there are differences of administrations, but the same Lord.

And there are diversities of operations, but it is the same God which worketh all in all.

But the manifestation of the Spirit is given to every man to profit withal.

For to one is given by the Spirit the word of wisdom; to another the word of knowledge by the same Spirit;

To another faith by the same Spirit; to another the gifts of healing by the same Spirit;

To another the working of miracles; to another prophecy; to another discerning of spirits; to another divers kinds of tongues; to another the interpretation of tongues:

But all these worketh that one and the selfsame Spirit, dividing to every man severally as he will.

For as the body is one, and hath many members, and all the members of that one body, being many, are one body: so also is Christ.

For by one Spirit are we all baptized into one body, whether we be Jews or Gentiles, whether we be bond or free; and have been all made to drink into one Spirit.

—*1 Corinthians 12:1–13*

For as we have many members in one body, and all members have not the same office:

So we, being many, are one body in Christ, and every one members one of another.

Having then gifts differing according to the grace that is given to us, whether prophecy, let us prophesy according to the proportion of faith;

Or ministry, let us wait on our ministering: or he that teacheth, on teaching;

Or he that exhorteth, on exhortation: he that giveth, let him do it with simplicity; he that ruleth, with diligence; he that sheweth mercy, with cheerfulness.

Let love be without dissimulation. Abhor that which is evil; cleave to that which is good.

Be kindly affectioned one to another with brotherly love; in honour preferring one another;

Not slothful in business; fervent in spirit; serving the Lord;

Rejoicing in hope; patient in tribulation; continuing instant in prayer;

Distributing to the necessity of saints; given to hospitality.

Bless them which persecute you: bless, and curse not.

Rejoice with them that do rejoice, and weep with them that weep.

Be of the same mind one toward another. Mind not high things, but condescend to men of low estate. Be not wise in your own conceits.

Recompense to no man evil for evil. Provide things honest in the sight of all men.

If it be possible, as much as lieth in you, live peaceably with all men.

—*Romans 12:4–18*

For the body is not one member, but many.

If the foot shall say, Because I am not the hand, I am not of the body; is it therefore not of the body?

And if the ear shall say, Because I am not the eye, I am not of the body; is it therefore not of the body?

If the whole body were an eye, where were the hearing? If the whole were hearing, where were the smelling?

But now hath God set the members every one of them in the body, as it hath pleased him.

And if they were all one member, where were the body?

But now are they many members, yet but one body.

And the eye cannot say unto the hand, I have no need of thee: nor again the head to the feet, I have no need of you.

Nay, much more those members of the body, which seem to be more feeble, are necessary:

And those members of the body, which we think to be less honourable, upon these we bestow more abundant honour; and our uncomely parts have more abundant comeliness.

For our comely parts have no need: but God hath tempered the body together, having given more abundant honour to that part which lacked:

That there should be no schism in the body; but that the members should have the same care one for another.

And whether one member suffer, all the members suffer with it; or one member be honoured, all the members rejoice with it.

—*1 Corinthians 12:14–26*

Now ye are the body of Christ, and members in particular.

And God hath set some in the church, first apostles, secondarily prophets, thirdly teachers, after that miracles, then gifts of healings, helps, governments, diversities of tongues.

Are all apostles? are all prophets? are all teachers? are all workers of miracles?

Have all the gifts of healing? do all speak with tongues? do all interpret?

But covet earnestly the best gifts: and yet shew I unto you a more excellent way.

—*1 Corinthians 12:27–31*

And he gave some, apostles; and some, prophets; and some, evangelists; and some, pastors and teachers;

For the perfecting of the saints, for the work of the ministry, for the edifying of the body of Christ.

—*Ephesians 4:11–12*

So Give Yourself to God's Will

Would you know who is the greatest saint in the world? It is not he who prays most or fasts most; it is not he who gives most alms, or is more eminent for temperance, chastity, or justice; but it is he who is always thankful to God, who wills everything that God wills, who receives everything as an instance of God's goodness, and has a heart always ready to praise God for it.

—William Law

I am thy servant; give me understanding, that I may know thy testimonies.

—Psalm 119:125

The kingdom of heaven is like unto treasure hid in a field; the which when a man hath found, he hideth, and for joy thereof goeth and selleth all that he hath, and buyeth that field.

Again, the kingdom of heaven is like unto a merchant man, seeking goodly pearls:

Who, when he had found one pearl of great price, went and sold all that he had, and bought it.

—*Matthew 13:44–46*

Neither yield ye your members as instruments of unrighteousness unto sin: but yield yourselves unto God, as those that are alive from the dead, and your members as instruments of righteousness unto God.

For sin shall not have dominion over you: for ye are not under the law, but under grace.

What then? shall we sin, because we are not under the law, but under grace? God forbid.

Know ye not, that to whom ye yield yourselves servants to obey, his servants ye are to whom ye obey; whether of sin unto death, or of obedience unto righteousness?

But God be thanked, that ye were the servants of sin, but ye have obeyed from the heart that form of doctrine which was delivered you.

Being then made free from sin, ye became the servants of righteousness.

I speak after the manner of men because of the infirmity of your flesh: for as ye have yielded your members servants to uncleanness and to iniquity unto iniquity; even so now yield your members servants to righteousness unto holiness.

—Romans 6:13–19

And this they did, not as we hoped, but first gave their own selves to the Lord, and unto us by the will of God.

—2 Corinthians 8:5

Christ's Power Will Sustain You

Verily, verily, I say unto you, He that believeth on me, the works that I do shall he do also; and greater works than these shall he do; because I go unto my Father.

—John 14:12

And he ordained twelve, that they should be with him, and that he might send them forth to preach,

And to have power to heal sicknesses, and to cast out devils.

—Mark 3:14–15

And the seventy returned again with joy, saying, Lord, even the devils are subject unto us through thy name.

And he said unto them, I beheld Satan as lightning fall from heaven.

Behold, I give unto you power to tread on serpents and scorpions, and over all the power of the enemy: and nothing shall by any means hurt you.

Notwithstanding in this rejoice not, that the spirits are subject unto you; but rather rejoice, because your names are written in heaven.

—Luke 10:17–20

But Don't Let Sin Hinder You

For the weapons of our warfare are not carnal, but mighty through God to the pulling down of strong holds.

—2 Corinthians 10:4

Now I Paul myself beseech you by the meekness and gentleness of Christ, who in presence am base among you, but being absent am bold toward you:

But I beseech you, that I may not be bold when I am present with that confidence, wherewith I think to be bold against some, which think of us as if we walked according to the flesh.

For though we walk in the flesh, we do not war after the flesh:

(For the weapons of our warfare are not carnal, but mighty through God to the pulling down of strong holds;)

Casting down imaginations, and every high thing that exalteth itself against the knowledge of God, and bringing into captivity every thought to the obedience of Christ;

And having in a readiness to revenge all disobedience, when your obedience is fulfilled.

Do ye look on things after the outward appearance? If any man trust to himself that he is Christ's, let him of himself think this again, that, as he is Christ's, even so are we Christ's.

For though I should boast somewhat more of our authority, which the Lord hath given us for edification, and not for your destruction, I should not be ashamed.

—2 Corinthians 10:1–8

Put on the whole armour of God, that ye may be able to stand against the wiles of the devil.

For we wrestle not against flesh and blood, but against principalities, against powers, against the rulers of the darkness of this world, against spiritual wickedness in high places.

Wherefore take unto you the whole armour of God, that ye may be able to withstand in the evil day, and having done all, to stand.

Stand therefore, having your loins girt about with truth, and having on the breastplate of righteousness.

—Ephesians 6:11–14

And the Lord shall deliver me from every evil work, and will preserve me unto his heavenly kingdom: to whom be glory for ever and ever.

—*2 Timothy 4:18*

Forasmuch then as the children are partakers of flesh and blood, he also himself likewise took part of the same; that through death he might destroy him that had the power of death, that is, the devil;

And deliver them who through fear of death were all their lifetime subject to bondage.

For verily he took not on him the nature of angels; but he took on him the seed of Abraham.

Wherefore in all things it behoved him to be made like unto his brethren, that he might be a merciful and faithful high priest in things pertaining to God, to make reconciliation for the sins of the people.

For in that he himself hath suffered being tempted, he is able to succour them that are tempted. . . .

Wherefore, holy brethren, partakers of the heavenly calling, consider the Apostle and High Priest of our profession, Christ Jesus.

—Hebrews 2:14–18; 3:1

Then saith he unto them, My soul is exceeding sorrowful, even unto death: tarry ye here, and watch with me.

And he went a little farther, and fell on his face, and prayed, saying, O my Father, if it be possible, let this cup pass from me: nevertheless not as I will, but as thou wilt.

And he cometh unto the disciples, and findeth them asleep, and saith unto Peter, What, could ye not watch with me one hour?

Watch and pray, that ye enter not into temptation: the spirit indeed is willing, but the flesh is weak.

—Matthew 26:38–41

And Keep Praying for Guidance

Man's goings are of the LORD; how can a man then understand his own way?

—Proverbs 20:24

Thus saith the LORD, thy Redeemer, the Holy One of Israel; I am the LORD thy God which teacheth thee to profit, which leadeth thee by the way that thou shouldest go.

O that thou hadst hearkened to my commandments! then had thy peace been as a river, and thy righteousness as the waves of the sea.

—Isaiah 48:17–18

A new heart also will I give you, and a new spirit will I put within you: and I will take away the stony heart out of your flesh, and I will give you an heart of flesh.

And I will put my spirit within you, and cause you to walk in my statutes, and ye shall keep my judgments, and do them.

—Ezekiel 36:26–27

And Israel took his journey with all that he had, and came to Beer–sheba, and offered sacrifices unto the God of his father Isaac.

And God spake unto Israel in the visions of the night, and said, Jacob, Jacob. And he said, Here am I.

And he said, I am God, the God of thy
father: fear not to go down into Egypt; for I
will there make of thee a great nation:

I will go down with thee into Egypt; and I
will also surely bring thee up again: and
Joseph shall put his hand upon thine eyes.

—*Genesis 46:1–4*

And it was told the king of Egypt that the
people fled: and the heart of Pharaoh and of
his servants was turned against the people,
and they said, Why have we done this, that
we have let Israel go from serving us?

And he made ready his chariot, and took
his people with him:

And he took six hundred chosen chariots,
and all the chariots of Egypt, and captains
over every one of them.

And the LORD hardened the heart of
Pharaoh king of Egypt, and he pursued
after the children of Israel: and the children
of Israel went out with an high hand.

But the Egyptians pursued after them, all
the horses and chariots of Pharaoh, and his
horsemen, and his army, and overtook them

encamping by the sea, beside Pi–hahiroth, before Baal–zephon.

And when Pharaoh drew nigh, the children of Israel lifted up their eyes, and, behold, the Egyptians marched after them; and they were sore afraid: and the children of Israel cried out unto the LORD.

And they said unto Moses, Because there were no graves in Egypt, hast thou taken us away to die in the wilderness? wherefore hast thou dealt thus with us, to carry us forth out of Egypt?

Is not this the word that we did tell thee in Egypt, saying, Let us alone, that we may serve the Egyptians? For it had been better for us to serve the Egyptians, than that we should die in the wilderness.

And Moses said unto the people, Fear ye not, stand still, and see the salvation of the LORD, which he will shew to you to day: for the Egyptians whom ye have seen to day, ye shall see them again no more for ever.

The LORD shall fight for you, and ye shall hold your peace.

—*Exodus 14:5–14*

And it came to pass after this, that David enquired of the LORD, saying, Shall I go up into any of the cities of Judah? And the LORD said unto him, Go up. And David said, Whither shall I go up? And he said, Unto Hebron.

So David went up thither, and his two wives also, Ahinoam the Jezreelitess, and Abigail Nabal's wife the Carmelite.

And his men that were with him did David bring up, every man with his household: and they dwelt in the cities of Hebron.

And the men of Judah came, and there they anointed David king over the house of Judah. And they told David, saying, That the men of Jabesh–gilead were they that buried Saul.

—*2 Samuel 2:1–4*

David perceived that the LORD had established him king over Israel, and that he had exalted his kingdom for his people Israel's sake.

And David took him more concubines and wives out of Jerusalem, after he was come from Hebron: and there were yet sons and daughters born to David.

And these be the names of those that were born unto him in Jerusalem; Shammuah, and Shobab, and Nathan, and Solomon,

Ibhar also, and Elishua, and Nepheg, and Japhia,

And Elishama, and Eliada, and Eliphalet.

But when the Philistines heard that they had anointed David king over Israel, all the Philistines came up to seek David; and David heard of it, and went down to the hold.

The Philistines also came and spread themselves in the valley of Rephaim.

And David enquired of the LORD, saying, Shall I go up to the Philistines? wilt thou deliver them into mine hand? And the LORD said unto David, Go up: for I will doubtless deliver the Philistines into thine hand.

—*2 Samuel 5:12–19*

Thy word is a lamp unto my feet, and a light unto my path. . . .

I am thy servant; give me understanding,
that I may know thy testimonies.

—Psalm 119:105, 125

Now there were in the church that was at
Antioch certain prophets and teachers; as
Barnabas, and Simeon that was called Niger,
and Lucius of Cyrene, and Manaen, which
had been brought up with Herod the
tetrarch, and Saul.

As they ministered to the Lord, and
fasted, the Holy Ghost said, Separate me
Barnabas and Saul for the work whereunto I
have called them.

And when they had fasted and prayed,
and laid their hands on them, they sent
them away.

—Acts 13:1–3

Then spake the Lord to Paul in the night
by a vision, Be not afraid, but speak, and
hold not thy peace:

For I am with thee, and no man shall set
on thee to hurt thee: for I have much people
in this city.

And he continued there a year and six months, teaching the word of God among them.

—*Acts 18:9–11*

Nine

Does God Care About My Health?

Of course God cares about your health! We are much more then disembodied intelligences. He made us whole—body, soul, and spirit. When the body isn't healthy, God cares. That's not to say, of course, that we can't learn some valuable lessons through illness—like patience, courage, and perseverance. However, when all

*is said and done, we remain responsible for
keeping our bodies in the best shape they can
be.*

Yes, God Cares About the Whole Person

*One should hallow all that one does in one's
natural life. One eats in holiness, tastes the
taste of food in holiness, and the table
becomes an altar. One works in holiness, and
he raises up the sparks which hide
themselves in all tools. One walks in holiness
across the fields, and the soft songs of all
herbs, which they voice to God, enter into
the song of our soul.*

—*Martin Buber*[1]

When the morning was now come, Jesus
stood on the shore: but the disciples knew
not that it was Jesus.

Then Jesus saith unto them, Children,
have ye any meat? They answered him, No.

And he said unto them, Cast the net on the right side of the ship, and ye shall find. They cast therefore, and now they were not able to draw it for the multitude of fishes.

Therefore that disciple whom Jesus loved saith unto Peter, It is the Lord. Now when Simon Peter heard that it was the Lord, he girt his fisher's coat unto him, (for he was naked,) and did cast himself into the sea.

And the other disciples came in a little ship; (for they were not far from land, but as it were two hundred cubits,) dragging the net with fishes.

As soon then as they were come to land, they saw a fire of coals there, and fish laid thereon, and bread.

Jesus saith unto them, Bring of the fish which ye have now caught.

Simon Peter went up, and drew the net to land full of great fishes, an hundred and fifty and three: and for all there were so many, yet was not the net broken.

Jesus saith unto them, Come and dine. And none of the disciples durst ask him, Who art thou? knowing that it was the Lord.

Jesus then cometh, and taketh bread, and giveth them, and fish likewise.

This is now the third time that Jesus shewed himself to his disciples, after that he was risen from the dead.

—*John 21:4–14*

For we are his workmanship, created in Christ Jesus unto good works, which God hath before ordained that we should walk in them.

—*Ephesians 2:10*

So God created man in his own image, in the image of God created he him; male and female created he them.

And God blessed them, and God said unto them, Be fruitful, and multiply, and replenish the earth, and subdue it: and have dominion over the fish of the sea, and over the fowl of the air, and over every living thing that moveth upon the earth.

And God said, Behold, I have given you every herb bearing seed, which is upon the face of all the earth, and every tree, in the which is the fruit of a tree yielding seed; to you it shall be for meat.

And to every beast of the earth, and to every fowl of the air, and to every thing that creepeth upon the earth, wherein there is life, I have given every green herb for meat: and it was so.

And God saw every thing that he had made, and, behold, it was very good. And the evening and the morning were the sixth day.

—Genesis 1:27–31

I will praise thee; for I am fearfully and wonderfully made: marvellous are thy works; and that my soul knoweth right well.

My substance was not hid from thee, when I was made in secret, and curiously wrought in the lowest parts of the earth.

Thine eyes did see my substance, yet being unperfect; and in thy book all my members were written, which in continuance were fashioned, when as yet there was none of them.

—Psalm 139:14–16

I beseech you therefore, brethren, by the mercies of God, that ye present your bodies a living sacrifice, holy, acceptable unto God, which is your reasonable service.

—*Romans 12:1*

What? know ye not that your body is the temple of the Holy Ghost which is in you, which ye have of God, and ye are not your own?

For ye are bought with a price: therefore glorify God in your body, and in your spirit, which are God's.

—*1 Corinthians 6:19–20*

For our conversation is in heaven; from whence also we look for the Saviour, the Lord Jesus Christ:

Who shall change our vile body, that it may be fashioned like unto his glorious body, according to the working whereby he is able even to subdue all things unto himself.

—*Philippians 3:20–21*

Take Care of Your Body

Look to your health; and if you have it, praise God, and value it next to a good conscience. For health is the second blessing that we mortals are capable of—a blessing that money cannot buy.

—Izaak Walton

I wish above all things that thou mayest prosper and be in health, even as thy soul prospereth.

—3 John 2

Get Enough Rest

Six days thou shalt do thy work, and on the seventh day thou shalt rest: that thine ox and thine ass may rest, and the son of thy handmaid, and the stranger, may be refreshed.

—Exodus 23:12

And the apostles gathered themselves together unto Jesus, and told him all things, both what they had done, and what they had taught.

And he said unto them, Come ye yourselves apart into a desert place, and rest a while: for there were many coming and going, and they had no leisure so much as to eat.

And they departed into a desert place by ship privately.

—Mark 6:30–31

I laid me down and slept; I awaked; for the LORD sustained me.

—Psalm 3:5

Stand in awe, and sin not: commune with your own heart upon your bed, and be still.

—Psalm 4:4

Offer the sacrifices of righteousness, and put your trust in the LORD.

There be many that say, Who will shew us any good? LORD, lift thou up the light of thy countenance upon us.

Thou hast put gladness in my heart, more than in the time that their corn and their wine increased.

I will both lay me down in peace, and sleep: for thou, LORD, only makest me dwell in safety.

—Psalm 4:5–8

ℰ*Make Time for Exercise*

Know ye not that ye are the temple of God, and that the Spirit of God dwelleth in you?

If any man defile the temple of God, him shall God destroy; for the temple of God is holy, which temple ye are.

—1 Corinthians 3:16–17

For no man ever yet hated his own flesh; but nourisheth and cherisheth it, even as the Lord the church.

—Ephesians 5:29

Watch Your Nutrition

But Daniel proposed in his heart that he would not defile himself with the portion of the king's meat, nor with the wine which he drank: therefore he requested of the prince of the eunuchs that he might not defile himself.

Now God had brought Daniel into favour and tender love with the prince of the eunuchs.

And the prince of the eunuchs said unto Daniel, I fear my lord the king, who hath appointed your meat and your drink: for why should he see your faces worse liking than the children which are of your sort? then shall ye make me endanger my head to the king.

Then said Daniel to Melzar, whom the prince of the eunuchs had set over Daniel, Hananiah, Mishael, and Azariah,

Prove thy servants, I beseech thee, ten days: and let them give us pulse to eat, and water to drink.

Then let our countenances be looked upon before thee, and the countenance of the children that eat of the portion of the king's meat: and as thou seest, deal with thy servants.

So he consented to them in this matter, and proved them ten days.

And at the end of ten days their countenances appeared fairer and fatter in flesh than all the children which did eat the portion of the king's meat.

Thus Melzar took away the portion of their meat, and the wine that they should drink; and gave them pulse.

As for these four children, God gave them knowledge and skill in all learning and wisdom: and Daniel had understanding in all visions and dreams.

Now at the end of the days that the king had said he should bring them in, then the prince of the eunuchs brought them in before Nebuchadnezzar.

And the king communed with them; and among them all was found none like Daniel, Hananiah, Mishael, and Azariah: therefore stood they before the king.

And in all matters of wisdom and understanding, that the king enquired of them, he found them ten times better than all the magicians and astrologers that were in all his realm.

—*Daniel 1:8–20*

✐Trust in God's Strength

Where wast thou when I laid the foundations of the earth? declare, if thou hast understanding.

Who hath laid the measures thereof, if thou knowest? or who hath stretched the line upon it?

Whereupon are the foundations thereof fastened? or who laid the corner stone thereof;

When the morning stars sang together, and all the sons of God shouted for joy?

Or who shut up the sea with doors, when it brake forth, as if it had issued out of the womb?

When I made the cloud the garment thereof, and thick darkness a swaddlingband for it,

And brake up for it my decreed place, and set bars and doors,

And said, Hitherto shalt thou come, but no further: and here shall thy proud waves be stayed?

Hast thou commanded the morning since thy days; and caused the dayspring to know his place;

That it might take hold of the ends of the earth, that the wicked might be shaken out of it?

It is turned as clay to the seal; and they stand as a garment.

And from the wicked their light is withholden, and the high arm shall be broken.

Hast thou entered into the springs of the sea? or hast thou walked in the search of the depth?

Have the gates of death been opened unto thee? or hast thou seen the doors of the shadow of death?

Hast thou perceived the breadth of the earth? declare if thou knowest it all.

Where is the way where light dwelleth? and as for darkness, where is the place thereof,

That thou shouldest take it to the bound thereof, and that thou shouldest know the paths to the house thereof?

Knowest thou it, because thou wast then born? or because the number of thy days is great?

Hast thou entered into the treasures of the snow? or hast thou seen the treasures of the hail,

Which I have reserved against the time of trouble, against the day of battle and war?

By what way is the light parted, which scattereth the east wind upon the earth?

Who hath divided a watercourse for the overflowing of waters, or a way for the lightning of thunder;

To cause it to rain on the earth, where no man is; on the wilderness, wherein there is no man;

To satisfy the desolate and waste ground; and to cause the bud of the tender herb to spring forth?

—Job 38:4–27

Cut Down on Bad Habits

Who can understand his errors? cleanse thou me from secret faults.

Keep back thy servant also from presumptuous sins; let them not have dominion over me: then shall I be upright, and I shall be innocent from the great transgression.

Let the words of my mouth, and the meditation of my heart, be acceptable in thy sight, O LORD, my strength, and my redeemer.

—Psalm 19:12–14

And if thy right eye offend thee, pluck it out, and cast it from thee: for it is profitable for thee that one of thy members should perish, and not that thy whole body should be cast into hell.

And if thy right hand offend thee, cut if off, and cast it from thee: for it is profitable for thee that one of thy members should perish, and not that thy whole body should be cast into hell.

—*Matthew 5:29–30*

But fornication, and all uncleanness, or covetousness, let it not be once named among you, as becometh saints;

Neither filthiness, nor foolish talking, nor jesting, which are not convenient: but rather giving of thanks.

For this ye know, that no whoremonger, nor unclean person, nor covetous man, who is an idolater, hath any inheritance in the kingdom of Christ and of God.

Let no man deceive you with vain words: for because of these things cometh the wrath of God upon the children of disobedience.

Be not ye therefore partakers with them.

And be not drunk with wine, wherein is excess; but be filled with the Spirit;

—*Ephesians 5:3–7, 18*

Remember now thy Creator in the days of thy youth, while the evil days come not, nor the years draw nigh, when thou shalt say, I have no pleasure in them;

While the sun, or the light, or the moon, or the stars, be not darkened, nor the clouds return after the rain:

In the day when the keepers of the house shall tremble, and the strong men shall bow themselves, and the grinders cease because they are few, and those that look out of the windows be darkened,

And the doors shall be shut in the streets, when the sound of the grinding is low, and he shall rise up at the voice of the bird, and all the daughters of musick shall be brought low;

Also when they shall be afraid of that which is high, and fears shall be in the way, and the almond tree shall flourish, and the grasshopper shall be a burden, and desire shall fail: because man goeth to his long home, and the mourners go about the streets:

Or ever the silver cord be loosed, or the golden bowl be broken, or the pitcher be broken at the fountain, or the wheel broken at the cistern.

Then shall the dust return to the earth as
it was: and the spirit shall return unto God
who gave it.

—*Ecclesiastes 12:1–7*

That ye might walk worthy of the Lord
unto all pleasing, being fruitful in every
good work, and increasing in the knowledge
of God;

Strengthened with all might, according to
his glorious power, unto all patience and
longsuffering with joyfulness;

Giving thanks unto the Father, which
hath made us meet to be partakers of the
inheritance of the saints in light.

—*Colossians 1:10–12*

Love not the world, neither the things
that are in the world. If any man love the
world, the love of the Father is not in him.

For all that is in the world, the lust of the
flesh, and the lust of the eyes, and the pride
of life, is not of the Father, but is of the
world.

And the world passeth away, and the lust thereof: but he that doeth the will of God abideth for ever.

—*1 John 2:15–17*

Seek God's Healing Power

For I will restore health unto thee, and I will heal thee of thy wounds, saith the LORD; because they called thee an Outcast, saying, This is Zion, whom no man seeketh after.

—*Jeremiah 30:17*

Then the eyes of the blind shall be opened, and the ears of the deaf shall be unstopped.

Then shall the lame man leap as an hart, and the tongue of the dumb sing: for in the wilderness shall waters break out, and streams in the desert.

—*Isaiah 35:5–6*

When the even was come, they brought unto him many that were possessed with devils: and he cast out the spirits with his word, and healed all that were sick:

That it might be fulfilled which was spoken by Esaias the prophet, saying, Himself took our infirmities, and bare our sicknesses.

—*Matthew 8:16–17*

And as the lame man which was healed held Peter and John, all the people ran together unto them in the porch that is called Solomon's, greatly wondering.

And when Peter saw it, he answered unto the people, Ye men of Israel, why marvel ye at this? or why look ye so earnestly on us, as though by our own power or holiness we had made this man to walk?

The God of Abraham, and of Isaac, and of Jacob, the God of our fathers, hath glorified his Son Jesus; whom ye delivered up, and denied him in the presence of Pilate, when he was determined to let him go.

But ye denied the Holy One and the Just, and desired a murderer to be granted unto you;

And killed the Prince of life, whom God hath raised from the dead; whereof we are witnesses.

And his name through faith in his name hath made this man strong, whom ye see and know: yea, the faith which is by him hath given him this perfect soundness in the presence of you all.

—Acts 3:11–16

And in that same hour he cured many of their infirmities and plagues, and of evil spirits; and unto many that were blind he gave sight.

Then Jesus answering said unto them, Go your way, and tell John what things ye have seen and heard; how that the blind see, the lame walk, the lepers are cleansed, the deaf hear, the dead are raised, to the poor the gospel is preached.

And blessed is he, whosoever shall not be offended in me.

—Luke 7:21–23

And God hath set some in the church, first apostles, secondarily prophets, thirdly teachers, after that miracles, then gifts of healings, helps, governments, diversities of tongues.

Are all apostles? are all prophets? are all teachers? are all workers of miracles?

Have all the gifts of healing? do all speak with tongues? do all interpret?

But covet earnestly the best gifts: and yet shew I unto you a more excellent way.

—*1 Corinthians 12:28–31*

Is any among you afflicted? let him pray. Is any merry? let him sing psalms.

Is any sick among you? let him call for the elders of the church; and let them pray over him, anointing him with oil in the name of the Lord:

And the prayer of faith shall save the sick, and the Lord shall raise him up; and if he have committed sins, they shall be forgiven him.

—*James 5:13–15*

Ten

How Can I Improve My Attitude Today?

Someone once said: "My interpretations are my world." There's a sense in which it's true. After all, we can't control the kind of world we have on a daily basis, but we can control how we judge the things that happen to us. Everything that happens is an event. Is it a

good event or a bad event? Ultimately only you
can decide. It's your life!

Learn to Be Thankful!

That gift of his, from God descended.

Ah! friend, what gift of man's does not?
—Robert Browning

Every good gift and every perfect gift is
from above, and cometh down from the
Father of lights, with whom is no
variableness, neither shadow of turning.
—*James 1:17*

In every thing give thanks: for this is the
will of God in Christ Jesus concerning you.
—*1 Thessalonians 5:18*

Then went king David in, and sat before
the LORD, and he said, Who am I, O Lord
GOD? and what is my house, that thou hast
brought me hitherto?
And this was yet a small thing in thy
sight, O Lord GOD; but thou hast spoken
also of thy servant's house for a great while

to come. And is this the manner of man, O Lord GOD?

And what can David say more unto thee? for thou, Lord GOD, knowest thy servant.

For thy word's sake, and according to thine own heart, hast thou done all these great things, to make thy servant know them.

Wherefore thou art great, O LORD God: for there is none like thee, neither is there any God beside thee, according to all that we have heard with our ears.

And what one nation in the earth is like thy people, even like Israel, whom God went to redeem for a people to himself, and to make him a name, and to do for you great things and terrible, for thy land, before thy people, which thou redeemedst to thee from Egypt, from the nations and their gods?

For thou hast confirmed to thyself thy people Israel to be a people unto thee for ever: and thou, LORD, art become their God.

And now, O LORD God, the word that thou hast spoken concerning thy servant, and concerning his house, establish it for ever, and do as thou hast said.

And let thy name be magnified for ever, saying, The LORD of hosts is the God over

Israel: and let the house of thy servant
David be established before thee.

For thou, O Lord of hosts, God of Israel,
hast revealed to thy servant, saying, I will
build thee an house: therefore hath thy
servant found in his heart to pray this
prayer unto thee.

And now, O Lord God, thou art that
God, and thy words be true, and thou hast
promised this goodness unto thy servant:

Therefore now let it please thee to bless
the house of thy servant, that it may
continue for ever before thee: for thou, O
Lord God, hast spoken it: and with thy
blessing let the house of thy servant be
blessed for ever.

—2 Samuel 7:18–29

And the king turned his face about, and
blessed all the congregation of Israel: (and
all the congregation of Israel stood;)

And he said, Blessed be the Lord God of
Israel, which spake with his mouth unto
David my father, and hath with his hand
fulfilled it, saying,

Since the day that I brought forth my
people Israel out of Egypt, I chose no city
out of all the tribes of Israel to build an

house, that my name might be therein; but I chose David to be over my people Israel.

And it was in the heart of David my father to build an house for the name of the LORD God of Israel.

And the LORD said unto David my father, Whereas it was in thine heart to build an house unto my name, thou didst well that it was in thine heart.

Nevertheless thou shalt not build the house; but thy son that shall come forth out of thy loins, he shall build the house unto my name.

And the LORD hath performed his word that he spake, and I am risen up in the room of David my father, and sit on the throne of Israel, as the LORD promised, and have built an house for the name of the LORD God of Israel.

And I have set there a place for the ark, wherein is the covenant of the LORD, which he made with our fathers, when he brought them out of the land of Egypt.

—1 Kings 8:14–21

Then was the secret revealed unto Daniel in a night vision. Then Daniel blessed the God of heaven.

Daniel answered and said, Blessed be the name of God for ever and ever: for wisdom and might are his:

And he changeth the times and the seasons: he removeth kings, and setteth up kings: he giveth wisdom unto the wise, and knowledge to them that know understanding:

He revealeth the deep and secret things: he knoweth what is in the darkness, and the light dwelleth with him.

I thank thee, and praise thee, O thou God of my fathers, who hast given me wisdom and might, and hast made known unto me now what we desired of thee: for thou hast now made known unto us the king's matter.

—*Daniel 2:19–23*

Be careful for nothing; but in every thing by prayer and supplication with thanksgiving let your requests be made known unto God.

—*Philippians 4:6*

Live In the Light of Heaven

For now we see through a glass, darkly; but then face to face: now I know in part; but then shall I know even as also I am known.

And now abideth faith, hope, charity, these three; but the greatest of these is charity.

—*1 Corinthians 13:12–13*

Let not your heart be troubled: ye believe in God, believe also in me.

In my Father's house are many mansions: if it were not so, I would have told you. I go to prepare a place for you.

And if I go and prepare a place for you, I will come again, and receive you unto myself; that where I am, there ye may be also.

And whither I go ye know, and the way ye know.

—*John 14:1–4*

There remaineth therefore a rest to the people of God.

—*Hebrews 4:9*

But ye are come unto mount Sion, and unto the city of the living God, the heavenly Jerusalem, and to an innumerable company of angels,

To the general assembly and church of the firstborn, which are written in heaven, and to God the Judge of all, and to the spirits of just men made perfect,

And to Jesus the mediator of the new covenant, and to the blood of sprinkling, that speaketh better things than that of Abel.

See that ye refuse not him that speaketh. For if they escaped not who refused him that spake on earth, much more shall not we escape, if we turn away from him that speaketh from heaven

Whose voice then shook the earth: but now he hath promised, saying, Yet once more I shake not the earth only, but also heaven.

And this word, Yet once more, signifieth the removing of those things that are shaken, as of things that are made, that those things which cannot be shaken may remain.

Wherefore we receiving a kingdom which cannot be moved, let us have grace, whereby we may serve God acceptably with reverence and godly fear.

—*Hebrews 12:22–28*

If ye then be risen with Christ, seek those things which are above, where Christ sitteth on the right hand of God.

Set your affection on things above, not on things on the earth.

For ye are dead, and your life is hid with Christ in God.

When Christ, who is our life, shall appear, then shall ye also appear with him in glory.

Mortify therefore your members which are upon the earth; fornication, uncleanness, inordinate affection, evil concupiscence, and covetousness, which is idolatry:

For which things' sake the wrath of God cometh on the children of disobedience:

In the which ye also walked some time, when ye lived in them.

But now ye also put off all these; anger, wrath, malice, blasphemy, filthy communication out of your mouth.

Lie not one to another, seeing that ye have put off the old man with his deeds.

—*Colossians 3:1–9*

Enjoy the Life He Has Given You

The LORD is the portion of mine
inheritance and of my cup: thou
maintainest my lot.

The lines are fallen unto me in pleasant
places; yea, I have a goodly heritage.

—*Psalm 16:5–6*

Then he said unto them, Go your way, eat
the fat, and drink the sweet, and send
portions unto them for whom nothing is
prepared: for this day is holy unto our Lord:
neither be ye sorry; for the joy of the LORD
is your strength. . . .

And all the congregation of them that
were come again out of the captivity made
booths, and sat under the booths: for since
the days of Jeshua the son of Nun unto that
day had not the children of Israel done so.
And there was very great gladness.

Also day by day, from the first day unto
the last day, he read in the book of the law
of God. And they kept the feast seven days;

and on the eighth day was a solemn
assembly, according unto the manner.

—*Nehemiah 8:10, 17–18*

Thou hast turned for me my mourning
into dancing: thou hast put off my
sackcloth, and girded me with gladness;
To the end that my glory may sing praise
to thee, and not be silent. O Lord my God, I
will give thanks unto thee for ever.

—*Psalm 30:11–12*

He maketh the barren woman to keep
house, and to be a joyful mother of
children. Praise ye the Lord.

—*Pslam 113:9*

They that sow in tears shall reap in joy.
He that goeth forth and weepeth, bearing
precious seed, shall doubtless come again
with rejoicing, bringing his sheaves with
him.

—*Psalm 126:5–6*

Sing, O ye heavens; for the Lord hath
done it: shout, ye lower parts of the earth:
break forth into singing, ye mountains, O
forest, and every tree therein: for the Lord

hath redeemed Jacob, and glorified himself
in Israel.

And when he cometh home, he calleth
together his friends and neighbours, saying
unto them, Rejoice with me; for I have
found my sheep which was lost.

I say unto you, that likewise joy shall be
in heaven over one sinner that repenteth,
more than over ninety and nine just
persons, which need no repentance.

Either what woman having ten pieces of
silver, if she lose one piece, doth not light a
candle, and sweep the house, and seek
diligently till she find it?

And when she hath found it, she calleth
her friends and her neighbours together,
saying, Rejoice with me; for I have found
the piece which I had lost.

Likewise, I say unto you, there is joy in
the presence of the angels of God over one
sinner that repenteth.

—Luke 15:6–10

Thou hast loved righteousness, and hated
iniquity; therefore God, even thy God, hath

anointed thee with the oil of gladness above
thy fellows.

—*Hebrews 1:9*

My brethren, count it all joy when ye fall
into divers temptations;

Knowing this, that the trying of your
faith worketh patience.

But let patience have her perfect work,
that ye may be perfect and entire, wanting
nothing.

If any of you lack wisdom, let him ask of
God, that giveth to all men liberally, and
upbraideth not; and it shall be given him.

But let him ask in faith, nothing
wavering. For he that wavereth is like a wave
of the sea driven with the wind and tossed.

—*James 1:2–6*

But rejoice, inasmuch as ye are partakers
of Christ's sufferings; that, when his glory
shall be revealed, ye may be glad also with
exceeding joy.

—*1 Peter 4:13*

Offer Praise and Worship Every Day

Wonder is the basis of worship.
> —*Thomas Carlyle*

O come, let us worship and bow down:
let us kneel before the LORD our maker.
> —*Psalm 95:6*

This is the day which the LORD hath
made; we will rejoice and be glad in it.
> —*Psalm 118:24*

Praise ye the LORD. Praise ye the name of
the LORD; praise him, O ye servants of the
LORD.

Ye that stand in the house of the LORD, in
the courts of the house of our God,

Praise the LORD; for the LORD is good:
sing praises unto his name; for it is pleasant.

For the LORD hath chosen Jacob unto
himself, and Israel for his peculiar treasure.

For I know that the LORD is great, and
that our Lord is above all gods.

Whatsoever the LORD pleased, that did he in heaven, and in earth, in the seas, and all deep places.

He causeth the vapours to ascend from the ends of the earth; he maketh lightnings for the rain; he bringeth the wind out of his treasuries.

Who smote the firstborn of Egypt, both of man and beast.

Who sent tokens and wonders into the midst of thee, O Egypt, upon Pharaoh, and upon all his servants.

Who smote great nations, and slew mighty kings;

Sihon king of the Amorites, and Og king of Bashan, and all the kingdoms of Canaan:

And gave their land for an heritage, an heritage unto Israel his people.

Thy name, O LORD, endureth for ever; and thy memorial, O LORD, throughout all generations.

For the LORD will judge his people, and he will repent himself concerning his servants.

The idols of the heathen are silver and gold, the work of men's hands.

They have mouths, but they speak not;
eyes have they, but they see not;

They have ears, but they hear not; neither
is there any breath in their mouths.

They that make them are like unto them:
so is every one that trusteth in them.

Bless the LORD, O house of Israel: bless
the LORD, O house of Aaron:

Bless the LORD, O house of Levi: ye that
fear the LORD, bless the LORD.

Blessed be the LORD out of Zion, which
dwelleth at Jerusalem. Praise ye the LORD.

—*Psalm 135*

I will praise thee with my whole heart:
before the gods will I sing praise unto thee.

I will worship toward thy holy temple,
and praise thy name for thy lovingkindness
and for thy truth: for thou hast magnified
thy word above all thy name.

In the day when I cried thou answeredst
me, and strengthenedst me with strength in
my soul.

All the kings of the earth shall praise
thee, O LORD, when they hear the words of
thy mouth.

Yea, they shall sing in the ways of the LORD: for great is the glory of the LORD.

Though the LORD be high, yet hath he respect unto the lowly: but the proud he knoweth afar off.

Though I walk in the midst of trouble, thou wilt revive me: thou shalt stretch forth thine hand against the wrath of mine enemies, and thy right hand shall save me.

The LORD will perfect that which concerneth me: thy mercy, O LORD, endureth for ever: forsake not the works of thine own hands.

—Psalm 138:1–8

I will sing of the mercies of the LORD for ever: with my mouth will I make known thy faithfulness to all generations.

For I have said, Mercy shall be built up for ever: thy faithfulness shalt thou establish in the very heavens.

I have made a covenant with my chosen, I have sworn unto David my servant,

Thy seed will I establish for ever, and build up thy throne to all generations.

—Psalm 89:1–4

The LORD shall increase you more and more, you and your children.

Ye are blessed of the LORD which made heaven and earth.

The heaven, even the heavens, are the LORD'S: but the earth hath he given to the children of men.

The dead praise not the LORD, neither any that go down into silence.

But we will bless the LORD from this time forth and for evermore. Praise the LORD.

—Psalm 115:14–18

I will extol thee, my God, O king; and I will bless thy name for ever and ever.

Every day will I bless thee; and I will praise thy name for ever and ever.

Great is the LORD, and greatly to be praised; and his greatness is unsearchable.

One generation shall praise thy works to another, and shall declare thy mighty acts.

—Psalm 145:1–4

Praise ye the LORD. Praise God in his sanctuary: praise him in the firmament of his power.

Praise him for his mighty acts: praise him according to his excellent greatness.

Praise him with the sound of the trumpet: praise him with the psaltery and harp.

Praise him with the timbrel and dance: praise him with stringed instruments and organs.

Praise him upon the loud cymbals: praise him upon the high sounding cymbals.

Let every thing that hath breath praise the LORD. Praise ye the LORD.

—*Psalm 150*

I will speak of the glorious honour of thy majesty, and of thy wondrous works.

And men shall speak of the might of thy terrible acts: and I will declare thy greatness.

They shall abundantly utter the memory of thy great goodness, and shall sing of thy righteousness.

The LORD is gracious, and full of compassion; slow to anger, and of great mercy.

The LORD is good to all: and his tender mercies are over all his works.

All thy works shall praise thee, O LORD; and thy saints shall bless thee.

They shall speak of the glory of thy kingdom, and talk of thy power;

To make known to the sons of men his mighty acts, and the glorious majesty of his kingdom.

Thy kingdom is an everlasting kingdom, and thy dominion endureth throughout all generations.

The LORD upholdeth all that fall, and raiseth up all those that be bowed down.

The eyes of all wait upon thee; and thou givest them their meat in due season.

Thou openest thine hand, and satisfiest the desire of every living thing.

The LORD is righteous in all his ways, and holy in all his works.

The LORD is nigh unto all them that call upon him, to all that call upon him in truth.

He will fulfil the desire of them that fear him: he also will hear their cry, and will save them.

The LORD preserveth all them that love him: but all the wicked will he destroy.

My mouth shall speak the praise of the
LORD: and let all flesh bless his holy name
for ever and ever.

—Psalm 145:5–21

Let the word of Christ dwell in you richly
in all wisdom; teaching and admonishing
one another in psalms and hymns and
spiritual songs, singing with grace in your
hearts to the Lord.

—Colossians 3:16

Notes

Chapter 2

1. Henri Nouwen, in *The Complete Book of Christian Prayer* (New York: Continuum Publishing Co., 1995).

Chapter 3

1. C.S. Lewis, *Mere Christianity* (New York: Macmillan, 1952).
2. Robert A. Cook, in Lloyd Cory, ed., *Quote, Unquote* (Wheaton: Scripture Press, 1977).
3. Unnatributted quotation in E. Paul Hovey (compiler), *the Treasury of Inspirational Anecodtes, Quotations, and Illustrations* (Grand Rapids: Fleming H. Revell, 1987).
4. E. Stanley Jones, Source unknown.

Chapter 4

1. Tim Stafford, *A Scruffy Husband Is a Happy Husband* (Colorado Springs: Focus on the Family, 1981).
2. George MacDonald, quoted in *Between Heaven and Earth* (San Francisco: Harper, 1997).
3. Jean Eudes, in *The Wisdom of the Saints* (New York: Oxford University Press, 1987).

4. C. S. Lewis, in a letter to Arthur Greeves.

Chapter 5

1. Dan Issel, in a WLS radio interview sound-bite, Chicago, IL, January, 1995.
2. Walter Trobisch, quoted in *Men's Devotional Bible* (Grand Rapids: Zondervan, 1993).

Chapter 6

1. Dave Barry, "What It Means to Be a Guy" (*Chicago Tribune Magazine*, April 30, 1995).
2. Mike Singletary, *Singletary on Singletary* (Nashville: Thomas Nelson, 1991).

Chapter 7

1. William Barclay, *Turning to God,* quoted in Keith Miller, *Habitation of Dragons* (Grand Rapids: Revell, 1993).
2. Paul Kroger, "Integrity at Work" (*New Man* magazine, Nov./Dec., 1994).

Chapter 8

1. Bill Hybels, *Honest to God?* (Grand Rapids: Zondervan, 1990).